AMERICA'S HEALTHY COOKING

chicken

AMERICA'S **HEALTHY COOKING**

chicken

JG
PRESS

Published by World Publications Group, Inc.
455 Somerset Avenue
North Dighton, MA 02764
www.wrldpub.net

All photographs courtesy of Sunset Books

ISBN 1-57215-415-2

Editors: Joel Carino and Emily Zelner
Designer: Lynne Yeamans/Lync
Production Director: Ellen Milionis

Printed and bound in China by SNP Leefung Printers Limited.

1 2 3 4 5   06 05 03 02

chicken

lemon chicken

preparation time: about 30 minutes

5 or 6 large lemons

³/4 cup plus 1 tablespoon cornstarch

¹/3 cup fat-free reduced-sodium chicken broth

¹/4 cup sugar

2 tablespoons light corn syrup

2 tablespoons distilled white vinegar

1 tablespoon plus 1 teaspoon vegetable oil

¹/2 teaspoon salt (optional)

2 cloves garlic, minced or pressed

2 large egg whites

¹/4 cup all-purpose flour

1 teaspoon baking powder

1 teaspoon finely minced fresh ginger

¹/8 teaspoon ground white pepper

1 pound skinless, boneless chicken breast, cut into ¹/2- by 3-inch strips

Finely shredded lemon peel

Cilantro sprigs

1 To prepare sauce, finely shred enough peel (colored part only) from 1 or 2 of the lemons to make ¹/2 teaspoon; set aside. Squeeze enough juice to measure 3 tablespoons. In a small bowl, stir together lemon juice and 1 tablespoon of the cornstarch until blended. Stir in lemon peel, broth, sugar, corn syrup, vinegar, 1 tablespoon water, 1 teaspoon of the oil, ¹/4 teaspoon of the salt (if using), and garlic. Set sauce aside.

2 Thinly slice the remaining lemons and place slices on a rimmed platter, overlapping them, if necessary; cover and set aside.

3 In a large bowl, beat egg whites and ¹/2 cup water to blend. Add remaining ³/4 cup cornstarch, flour, baking powder, ginger, remaining ¹/4 teaspoon salt (if using), and white pepper; stir until smoothly blended.

4 Heat remaining 1 tablespoon oil in a wide nonstick frying pan or wok over medium-high heat. Meanwhile, dip chicken pieces in egg-white batter. Lift out and drain briefly to let excess batter drip off; discard remaining batter.

5 When oil is hot, add chicken and stir-fry gently, separating pieces, until meat is lightly browned on outside and no longer pink in center; cut to test (5 to 7 minutes; if any pieces brown too much, remove them from pan and keep warm). Arrange chicken over lemon slices on platter; keep warm.

6 Wipe pan clean (be careful; pan is hot). Stir reserved lemon sauce well; pour into pan. Stir over medium-high heat until sauce boils and thickens slightly (1 to 2 minutes). Pour sauce over chicken and sprinkle with additional shredded lemon peel. Garnish with cilantro sprigs.

makes 4 servings

per serving: 368 calories, 30 g protein, 56 g carbohydrates, 6 g total fat, 66 mg cholesterol, 245 mg sodium

THAWING CHICKEN IN THE MICROWAVE: Unwrap a frozen 3- to 3 ¹/2- pound cut-up chicken, then place on a microwave-safe plate; cover loosely with heavy-duty plastic wrap. Microwave on MEDIUM (50%) for 10 minutes, turning chicken over and giving plate a quarter turn after 5 minutes. Let stand for 10 minutes. Repeat, microwaving and standing; as soon as possible, separate pieces and arrange in a single layer, with meatiest portions toward edge of plate. Wings should be thawed after second 10-minute period. Microwave remaining pieces on MEDIUM (50%) for 5 more minutes; let stand for 5 minutes. If needed, microwave on MEDIUM (50%) for 2 more minutes. Thawed chicken should be flexible, but still very cold.

peanut chicken with rice

preparation time: about 40 minutes

1 cup long-grain white rice

1 package (about 10 oz.) frozen tiny peas, thawed and drained

3 tablespoons crunchy or smooth peanut butter

3 tablespoons plum jam or grape jelly

1 1/2 teaspoons lemon juice

1 1/2 teaspoons reduced-sodium soy sauce

1 teaspoon Asian sesame oil

2 teaspoons vegetable oil mixed with teaspoon ground ginger

1 pound skinless, boneless chicken breast, cut into 54-inch pieces

2 tablespoons sliced green onion

Lemon wedges

1 In a 3- to 4-quart pan, bring 2 cups water to a boil over high heat; stir in rice. Reduce heat, cover, and simmer until liquid has been absorbed and rice is tender to bite (about 20 minutes). Stir peas into rice; remove from heat and keep warm. Fluff occasionally with a fork.

2 While rice is cooking, prepare sauce. In a small bowl, stir together peanut butter, jam, 2 tablespoons water, lemon juice, soy sauce, and sesame oil. Set aside.

3 Heat ginger oil in a wide nonstick frying pan or wok over medium-high heat. When oil is hot, add chicken and stir-fry until no longer pink in center; cut to test (4 to 6 minutes). Remove chicken from pan with a slotted spoon and keep warm. Discard drippings from pan and wipe pan clean (be careful; pan is hot).

4 Stir sauce well and pour into pan. Stir over medium heat just until smoothly blended and heated through. Add chicken and onion; remove pan from heat and stir to coat chicken and onion with sauce.

5 Spoon rice mixture onto a rimmed platter and top with chicken mixture. Offer lemon wedges to squeeze over stir-fry to taste.

makes 4 servings

per serving: 481 calories, 36 g protein, 58 g carbohydrates, 11 g total fat, 66 mg cholesterol, 312 mg sodium

chicken breasts calvados

preparation time: about 45 minutes

1 large Golden Delicious apple, peeled, cored, and thinly sliced

1/4 cup apple brandy, brandy, or apple juice

1/4 teaspoon ground nutmeg

2 skinless, boneless chicken breast halves (about 6 oz. *each*)

2 slices Havarti cheese (about 1 oz. *each*)

Chopped parsley

1 Divide apple slices between 2 shallow ovenproof 1 1/2- to 2-cup ramekins. Pour 2 tablespoons of the brandy into each ramekin, then sprinkle 1/8 teaspoon of the nutmeg evenly over apples. Cover ramekins tightly with foil and bake in a 400° oven until apples are tender when pierced (about 20 minutes).

2 Rinse chicken and pat dry. Place one piece in each ramekin; baste with cooking juices, then sprinkle evenly with remaining 1/8 teaspoon nutmeg. Bake, uncovered, until meat in thickest part is no longer pink; cut to test (about 12 minutes).

3 Top each chicken piece with a cheese slice. Broil 6 inches below heat until cheese is bubbly (about 2 minutes). Sprinkle with parsley.

makes 2 servings

per serving: 413 calories, 46 g protein, 15 g carbohydrates, 10 g total fat, 128 mg cholesterol, 324 mg sodium

mediterranean baked chicken & vegetables

preparation time: about 40 minutes

4 chicken breast halves (about 1 ³/₄ lbs. *total*), skinned and trimmed of fat

8 ounces mushrooms, sliced

1 pound zucchini, cut into ¹/₄-inch-thick slices

1 tablespoon olive oil

1 teaspoon *each* pepper and dry oregano

1 teaspoon fennel seeds, crushed

1 tablespoon dry basil

1 can (about 14 ¹/₂ oz.) pear-shaped tomatoes

Parsley sprigs

Grated Parmesan cheese

1 Rinse chicken, pat dry, and place in a 12- by 15-inch broiler pan. Arrange mushrooms and zucchini around chicken. Drizzle with oil. Sprinkle with pepper, oregano, fennel seeds, and basil; mix to coat chicken and vegetables with seasonings.

2 Cover pan tightly and bake in a 425° oven for 15 minutes. Cut up tomatoes, then stir tomatoes and their liquid into pan. Cover and continue to bake until meat near bone is no longer pink; cut to test (5 to 10 more minutes). Garnish with parsley sprigs; offer cheese to add to taste.

makes 4 servings

per serving: 230 calories , 34 g protein, 12 g carbohydrates, 6 g total fat 75 mg cholesterol, 258 mg sodium

apple country chicken

preparation time: about 55 minutes

1 teaspoon curry powder

1 large Golden Delicious apple, cored and chopped

1 large yellow onion, finely chopped

1 tablespoon lemon juice

4 ounces mushrooms, sliced

1 teaspoon chicken-flavored instant bouillon

2 cups apple juice or cider

3 ¹/₄ to 3 ¹/₂ pounds chicken thighs, skinned and trimmed of fat

1 tablespoon all-purpose flour

2 tablespoons sliced green onion

Plain low-fat yogurt or reduced-fat sour cream (optional)

1 Place curry powder in a wide frying pan and stir over medium heat until slightly darker in color (3 to 4 minutes). Add apple, yellow onion, lemon juice, mushrooms, bouillon, and 1 ½ cups of the apple juice. Increase heat to high and bring juice mixture to a boil.

2 Rinse chicken, pat dry, and add to pan. Then reduce heat, cover, and simmer until meat near bone is no longer pink; cut to test (about 30 minutes). Transfer chicken to a platter and keep warm.

3 In a small bowl, smoothly blend flour and remaining ½ cup apple juice. Gradually add to sauce in pan, stirring constantly; increase heat to high and cook, stirring, until sauce is thickened. Pour over chicken. Garnish with green onion; offer yogurt to add to taste, if desired.

makes 4 to 6 servings

per serving: 314 calories, 36 g protein, 25 g carbohydrates, 7 g total fat, 146 mg cholesterol, 380 mg sodium

raspberry-glazed turkey sauté

preparation time: about 35 minutes

3 green onions

¹/₃ cup seedless red raspberry jam or jelly

3 tablespoons raspberry or red wine vinegar

1 tablespoon Dijon mustard

¹/₂ teaspoon grated orange peel

³/₄ teaspoon chopped fresh tarragon or ¹/₄ teaspoon dried tarragon

8 ounces dried eggless spinach fettuccine or plain fettuccine

1 teaspoon olive oil or vegetable oil

2 turkey breast tenderloins (about 1 lb. *total*), cut into ¹/₄- by 2-inch strips

About 1 cup fresh raspberries

Tarragon sprigs

1 Trim and discard ends of onions. Cut onions into 2-inch lengths; then cut each piece lengthwise into slivers. Set aside. In a small bowl, stir together jam, vinegar, mustard, orange peel, and chopped tarragon; set aside.

2 In a 4- to 5-quart pan, cook fettuccine in about 8 cups boiling water until just tender to bite (8 to 10 minutes); or cook according to package directions.

3 Meanwhile, heat oil in a wide nonstick frying pan or wok over medium-high heat. When oil is hot, add turkey and 1 tablespoon water. Stir-fry just until turkey is no longer pink in center; cut to test (about 2 minutes). Add water, 1 table-spoon at a time, if pan appears dry. Remove turkey from pan with a slotted spoon and keep warm. Discard drippings from pan; wipe pan clean (be careful; pan is hot).

4 Add jam mixture to pan and bring to a boil over medium-high heat; then boil, stirring, just until jam is melted and sauce is smooth (about 1 minute). Remove from heat and stir in turkey and onions.

5 Drain pasta well and divide among 4 warm individual rimmed plates or shallow bowls; top with turkey mixture. Sprinkle each with raspberries and garnish with tarragon sprigs.

makes 4 servings

per serving: 435 calories, 36 g protein, 64 g carbohydrates, 3 g total fat, 70 mg cholesterol, 178 mg sodium

baked chicken with pears

preparation time: about 40 minutes

Vegetable oil cooking spray or salad oil

6 boneless, skinless chicken breast halves (about 2 ¹/₄ lbs. *total*)

3 tablespoons lemon juice

4 teaspoons cornstarch

1 cup pear-flavored brandy or apple juice

2 large red Bartlett or other firm-ripe pears (about 1 lb. *total*)

1 Lightly coat a 9- by 13-inch baking pan with cooking spray. Rinse chicken and pat dry; then rub with lemon juice and arrange, skinned side up, in pan. Bake in a 425° oven until meat in thickest part is no longer pink; cut to test (15 to 20 minutes).

2 Meanwhile, in a medium-size pan, smoothly blend cornstarch and brandy. Halve and core pears; cut lengthwise into ¹/₂-inch-thick slices. Add to brandy mixture and stir gently. Bring to a boil over medium-high heat; then reduce heat, cover, and simmer until pears are tender when pierced (about 5 minutes).

3 When chicken is done, pour pear mixture into baking pan; shake pan to mix gently. Transfer chicken and pears to individual plates; drizzle with sauce.

makes 6 servings

per serving: 348 calories, 40 g protein, 25 g carbohydrates, 3 g total fat, 99 mg cholesterol, 112 mg sodium

chicken chutney burgers

preparation time: about 15 minutes

2/3 cup Major Grey chutney, large pieces chopped

1 1/2 tablespoons lemon juice

1 tablespoon Dijon mustard

3/4 pound ground chicken

1/4 cup sliced green onion

1/2 teaspoon ground cumin

8 slices (*each* 1/2 in. thick) sourdough French bread

4 thin slices red onion

20 pre-washed spinach leaves

1 Combine chutney, lemon juice, and mustard; set two-thirds of mixture aside. Combine remaining chutney mixture with chicken, green onion, and cumin. Shape into 4 patties, each about 4 inches wide, and place on a rack in a broiler pan. Broil 3 inches below heat until well browned on both sides, turning as needed (6 to 7 minutes).

2 Meanwhile, brown bread in a toaster, then spread one side of each slice with reserved chutney mixture.

3 Separate red onion into rings and place between bread with burgers and spinach.

makes 4 servings

per serving: 387 calories, 23 g protein, 61 g carbohydrates, 4 g total fat, 60 mg cholesterol, 948 mg sodium

ground turkey chili mole

preparation time: about 1 hour

1 medium-size onion, chopped

1 pound ground skinless turkey

2 cloves garlic, minced or pressed

1 can (about 8 oz.) tomato sauce

1 can (about 14 1/2 oz.) stewed tomatoes

1 can (about 15 oz.) red kidney beans, drained and rinsed; or 2 cups cooked red kidney beans, drained and rinsed

1 tablespoon molasses

1/4 teaspoon liquid hot pepper seasoning

1 tablespoon unsweetened cocoa

1 teaspoon *each* paprika and ground cumin

1/2 teaspoon *each* dry oregano and dry basil

1 In a 4- to 5-quart pan, combine onion and 1/4 cup water. Bring to a boil over medium-high heat; then boil, stirring occasionally, until liquid evaporates and onion begins to brown (about 5 minutes). To deglaze, add 1/4 cup more water and stir to scrape browned bits free. Then continue to cook, stirring occasionally, until onion begins to brown again. Repeat deglazing and browning steps, using 1/4 cup more water.

2 Crumble turkey into pan; add garlic. Cook, stirring, until meat is no longer pink and liquid has evaporated. Stir in tomato sauce, tomatoes, beans, molasses, hot pepper seasoning, cocoa, paprika, cumin, oregano, and basil. Bring to a boil; reduce heat, cover, and simmer until flavors are well blended (about 30 minutes).

makes 4 to 6 servings

per serving: 256 calories, 22 g protein, 25 g carbohydrates, 8 g total fat, 66 mg cholesterol, 685 mg sodium

chicken and apple stir-fry

preparation time: about 35 minutes

4 teaspoons butter or margarine

2 large tart apples, peeled, cored, and cut into
^{1}/4-inch-thick slices

1 pound skinless, boneless chicken breast, cut into
^{1}/2- by 2-inch strips

1 large onion, finely chopped

^{2}/3 cup dry sherry or apple juice

^{1}/2 cup half-and-half

1 Melt 1 tablespoon of the butter in a wide nonstick frying pan or wok over medium heat. Add apples and stir-fry just until tender to bite (about 2 minutes). Remove apples from pan with a slotted spoon and keep warm.

2 Increase heat to medium-high and melt remaining 1 teaspoon butter in pan. Add chicken and stir-fry until no longer pink in center; cut to test (3 to 4 minutes). Remove chicken from pan with a slotted spoon and keep warm.

3 Add onion and 2 tablespoons of the sherry to pan; stir-fry until onion is soft (about 3 minutes). Add remaining sherry and bring to a boil; boil, stirring, for 1 minute. Add half-and-half and boil, stirring, until sauce is slightly thickened (about 2 minutes). Return apples and chicken to pan and mix gently but thoroughly.

makes 4 servings

per serving: 309 calories, 28 g protein, 21 g carbohydrates, 8 g total fat, 84 mg cholesterol, 126 mg sodium

braised chicken with green chile sauce

preparation time: about 55 minutes

1 large onion, chopped

2 cloves garlic, minced or pressed

1 cup low-sodium chicken broth

1 teaspoon dry oregano

^{1}/2 teaspoon ground cumin

1 tablespoon red wine vinegar

3 pounds boneless, skinless chicken or turkey thighs, trimmed of fat and cut into 1-inch chunks

2 large green bell peppers, seeded and chopped

^{1}/2 cup chopped cilantro

1 large can (about 7 oz.) diced green chiles

Salt and pepper

Hot cooked rice or warm flour tortillas

Tomato wedges, plain nonfat yogurt or reduced-fat sour cream, and lime wedges

1 In a 5- to 6-quart pan, combine onion, garlic, broth, oregano, and cumin. Bring to a boil over high heat; boil, stirring occasionally, until liquid evaporates and onion begins to brown (about 10 minutes). To deglaze, add 2 tablespoons water and stir to scrape browned bits free. Then continue to cook, stirring occasionally, until onion begins to brown again. Repeat deglazing and browning steps, using 2 tablespoons water each time, until onion is richly browned. Then deglaze one last time with vinegar and 1 tablespoon water.

2 Stir in chicken, bell peppers, cilantro, chiles, and 1 tablespoon water. Cover and cook over low heat, stirring often, until chicken chunks are no longer pink in center; cut to test (about 15 minutes). Skim and discard fat from sauce; season to taste with salt and pepper.

3 Spoon chicken mixture into a bowl. Serve over rice; offer tomato wedges, yogurt, and lime wedges to season each serving.

makes 6 to 8 servings

per serving: 273 calories, 40 g protein, 9 g carbohydrates, 8 g total fat, 161 mg cholesterol, 351 mg sodium

fig-stuffed turkey roast

preparation time: 1 1/2 hours

1 turkey breast half (about 3 1/2 lbs.), boned and skinned

3 tablespoons Dijon mustard

1 tablespoon chopped fresh rosemary or 1 teaspoon dried rosemary

12 dried Calimyrna or Mission figs, finely chopped

1 tablespoon honey

1 tablespoon olive oil

2 cloves garlic, minced

Pepper

Rosemary sprigs

1 Rinse turkey and pat dry. Then slice lengthwise down middle, cutting meat almost but not quite through. Push cut open and press turkey to make it lie as flat as possible. Spread turkey with mustard and sprinkle with half the chopped rosemary; set aside.

2 In a bowl, mix figs with honey. Mound fig mixture evenly down center of turkey. Starting from a long side, lift turkey and roll over filling to enclose. Tie roll snugly with cotton string at 2- to 3-inch intervals. Rub roll with oil, then with garlic; pat remaining chopped rosemary onto roll and sprinkle generously with pepper.

3 Place roll on a rack in a 9- by 13-inch baking pan; add 1/3 cup water to pan. Bake in a 375° oven until a meat thermometer inserted in thickest part of roll (insert thermometer in meat, not filling) registers 160° to 165°, about 1 1/4 hours. Add water, 1/4 cup at a time, if pan appears dry.

4 Remove roll from oven and let stand for 10 minutes; then snip and discard strings and cut roll crosswise into thick slices. Garnish with rosemary sprigs. Serve with pan juices, if desired.

makes 6 to 8 servings

per serving: 308 calories, 44 g protein, 24 g carbohydrates, 3 g total fat, 117 mg cholesterol, 232 mg sodium

plum chicken

preparation time: about 35 minutes

4 boneless, skinless chicken breast halves (about 1 1/2 lbs. *total*)

1 cup Asian plum sauce

1/4 cup minced onion

1 teaspoon grated lemon peel

2 tablespoons lemon juice

1 tablespoon reduced-sodium soy sauce

1/2 teaspoon *each* dry mustard and ground ginger

1/4 teaspoon *each* pepper and liquid hot pepper seasoning

1/4 teaspoon anise seeds, crushed

1 Rinse chicken and pat dry; then place, skinned side up, in a 9- by 13-inch baking pan. In a small bowl, stir together plum sauce, onion, lemon peel, lemon juice, soy sauce, mustard, ginger, pepper, hot pepper seasoning, and anise seeds.

2 Pour sauce evenly over chicken. Bake in a 400° oven, basting halfway through baking, until meat in thickest part is no longer pink; cut to test (about 25 minutes).

3 To serve, transfer chicken to a platter and spoon sauce over top.

makes 4 servings

per serving: 278 calories, 41 g protein, 23 g carbohydrates, 2 g total fat, 99 mg cholesterol, 581 mg sodium

salsa chicken

preparation time: about 30 minutes

2 medium-size tomatoes, chopped and drained well

¼ cup thinly sliced green onions

¼ cup lime juice

1 small fresh jalapeño chile, seeded and finely chopped

1 tablespoon chopped cilantro

1 clove garlic, minced or pressed

About 8 cups finely shredded iceberg lettuce

2 large egg whites

½ cup yellow cornmeal

1 ½ teaspoons chili powder

½ teaspoon ground cumin

1 pound skinless, boneless chicken breast, cut into 1-inch pieces

2 teaspoons olive oil or vegetable oil

½ cup nonfat sour cream

Cilantro sprigs

1 To prepare tomato salsa, in a large bowl, combine tomatoes, onions, lime juice, jalapeño, chopped cilantro, and garlic; set aside. (At this point, you may cover and refrigerate for up to 3 hours.) Divide lettuce among 4 individual plates; cover and set aside.

2 In a shallow bowl, beat egg whites to blend; set aside. In a large bowl, combine cornmeal, chili powder, and cumin. Add chicken and turn to coat. Then lift chicken from bowl, shaking off excess coating. Dip chicken into egg whites, then coat again with remaining cornmeal mixture.

3 Heat oil in a wide nonstick frying pan or wok over medium-high heat. When oil is hot, add chicken and stir-fry gently until no longer pink in center; cut to test (5 to 7 minutes). Remove from pan and keep warm. Pour reserved salsa into pan; reduce heat to medium and cook, stirring, until salsa is heated through and slightly thickened (1 to 2 minutes).

4 Arrange chicken over lettuce; top with salsa and sour cream. Garnish with cilantro sprigs.

makes 4 servings

per serving: 284 calories, 34 g protein, 26 g carbohydrates, 5 g total fat, 66 mg cholesterol, 152 mg sodium

chicken with pumpkin seeds

preparation time: about 35 minutes

4 chicken breast halves (about 1 ³/₄ lbs. *total*), skinned and trimmed of fat

¹/₃ cup roasted pumpkin seeds

1 can (about 4 oz.) diced green chiles

½ cup shredded jack cheese

Lime wedges

1 Rinse chicken and pat dry; then place, skinned side up, in a 9- by 13-inch baking pan. In a small bowl, mix pumpkin seeds, chiles, and cheese; pat evenly onto chicken.

2 Bake chicken in a 450° oven until meat near bone is no longer pink; cut to test (20 to 25 minutes). Serve with lime wedges.

makes 4 servings

per serving: 226 calories, 35 g protein, 5 g carbohydrates, 7 g total fat, 90 mg cholesterol, 334 mg sodium

spicy chicken tortas

preparation time: about 35 minutes

TORTAS:

1 pound skinless, boneless chicken thighs

2 cups fat-free reduced-sodium chicken broth

1/4 cup chili powder

1/4 cup firmly packed brown sugar

2 teaspoons dried oregano

1 teaspoon anise seeds

About 1 tablespoon red wine vinegar, or to taste

2 tablespoons chopped cilantro

2 tablespoons thinly sliced green onion

4 French rolls

8 to 12 butter lettuce leaves, rinsed and crisped

CONDIMENTS:

avocado slices

asadero or string cheese

1 Rinse chicken and pat dry; set aside. In a 4- to 5-quart pan with a tight-fitting lid, combine 4 cups water, broth, chili powder, sugar, oregano, and anise seeds. Bring to a rolling boil over high heat. Remove pan from heat and immediately add chicken. Cover pan and let stand until meat in thickest part is no longer pink; cut to test (15 to 20 minutes; do not uncover until ready to test). If chicken is not done, return it to hot water, cover, and let steep for 2 to 3 more minutes.

2 Drain chicken, reserving 2 cups of the cooking liquid. Return reserved liquid to pan. Bring to a boil over high heat; boil until reduced to 1/2 cup, watching closely to prevent scorching.

3 Serve chicken and sauce warm or cold. To serve, stir vinegar, cilantro, and onion into sauce. Cut chicken diagonally across the grain into thin slices; set aside. Cut rolls in half lengthwise and moisten cut surfaces evenly with sauce. Fill rolls with chicken and lettuce. Offer additional sauce and condiments to add to taste.

makes 4 servings

per serving: 464 calories, 33 g protein, 68 g carbohydrates, 7 g total fat, 94 mg cholesterol, 1,819 mg sodium

greek chicken pockets

preparation time: about 30 minutes

Herb Dressing (recipe follows)

4 to 6 pita breads (*each* about 6 inches in diameter)

3 small firm-ripe tomatoes, thinly sliced

2 small green bell peppers, seeded and thinly sliced

3 cups shredded cooked chicken

1/4 cup crumbled feta cheese

1 Prepare Herb Dressing.

2 Cut each pita bread in half; gently open halves and fill equally with tomatoes, bell peppers, chicken, and cheese. Then spoon dressing into each sandwich.

makes 4 to 6 servings

HERB DRESSING

In a small bowl, stir together 1 cup plain nonfat yogurt, 1/2 cup minced peeled cucumber, and 1 tablespoon each minced fresh dill and minced fresh mint (or 1 teaspoon each dry dill weed and dry mint).

per serving: 397 calories, 34 g protein, 44 g carbohydrates, 9 g total fat, 82 mg cholesterol, 512 mg sodium

chicken yakitori

preparation time: about 1 hour
marinating time: 1 to 8 hours

2 tablespoons sesame seeds

3 whole chicken breasts (about 1 lb. *each*), skinned, boned, and split

Sherry-Soy Marinade (recipe follows)

6 medium-size Asian eggplants

18 large fresh shiitake mushrooms or regular button mushrooms

1 In a small frying pan, toast sesame seeds over medium heat, shaking pan often, until golden (about 3 minutes). Set aside.

2 Cut each breast half into 6 equal-size chunks; place in a medium-size bowl, Prepare Sherry-Soy Marinade. Pour ¼ cup of the marinade over chicken, turning gently to coat; reserve remaining marinade. Cover and refrigerate chicken and reserved marinade separately for at least 1 hour or up to 8 hours.

3 Lift chicken from marinade and let drain briefly, discarding marinade in bowl. Thread chicken on skewers. Set aside.

4 Evenly slash each eggplant lengthwise in 4 or 5 places, making cuts about ⅓ inch deep. Cut mush room stems flush with caps. Place eggplants on a lightly greased grill 4 to 6 inches above a solid bed of hot coals. Cook, turning often, until very soft when pressed (about 35 minutes).

5 About 20 minutes before eggplants are done, dip mushrooms in reserved marinade, drain briefly, and place on grill. Cook, turning once, until lightly browned (about 10 minutes total). Meanwhile, place chicken on grill and cook, turning occasionally, until meat in center is no longer pink; cut to test (10 to 12 minutes).

6 Arrange chicken and vegetables on separate platters. Moisten with some of the remaining marinade and sprinkle with sesame seeds. Offer with remaining marinade.

makes 6 servings

SHERRY-SOY MARINADE

Stir together ⅓ cup dry sherry, 3 tablespoons *each* sesame oil and reduced sodium soy sauce, and 1 ½ teaspoons finely minced fresh ginger.

per serving: 295 calories, 39 g protein, 16 g carbohydrates, 9 g total fat, 86 mg cholesterol, 332 mg sodium

chicken and mushrooms with couscous

preparation time: about 40 minutes

1 pound skinless, boneless chicken thighs, trimmed of fat

1 tablespoon margarine

1 large onion, finely chopped

12 ounces mushrooms, sliced

2 teaspoons cornstarch

1 cup fat-free reduced-sodium chicken broth

3 tablespoons dry sherry

2 tablespoons soy sauce

1/8 teaspoon ground red pepper (cayenne)

2 cups low-fat (2%) milk

1 1/2 cups couscous

Vegetable oil cooking spray

Cilantro sprigs

1 Rinse chicken; pat dry. Place pieces between sheets of plastic wrap and pound with a flat-surfaced mallet until about 1/4 inch thick; then cut chicken into 1/2-inch-wide strips. Set aside.

2 Melt margarine in a wide nonstick frying pan over medium-high heat. Add onion and mushrooms; cook, stirring often, until liquid has evaporated and onion is golden and sweet tasting (10 to 12 minutes).

3 Meanwhile, in a bowl, blend cornstarch and 1/4 cup of the broth; stir in sherry, soy sauce, and red pepper. Set aside. In a 2-quart pan, bring milk and remaining 3/4 cup broth to a boil. Stir in couscous; cover, remove from heat, and let stand for 10 minutes.

4 Remove onion mixture from frying pan and set aside. Spray pan with cooking spray and place over high heat. Add chicken and cook, lifting and stirring, until meat is tinged with brown and is no longer pink in center; cut to test (4 to 5 minutes). Return onion mixture to pan; add cornstarch mixture and cook, stirring constantly, until sauce is bubbly (about 1 minute). Fluff couscous with a fork, then mound on a warm platter; spoon chicken beside couscous. Garnish with cilantro sprigs.

makes 4 to 6 servings

per serving: 446 calories, 31 g protein, 57 g carbohydrates, 9 g total fat, 83 mg cholesterol, 705 mg sodium

turkey chorizo sausage

preparation time: about 40 minutes
cooling time: at least 8 hours

1 large onion, chopped

2 teaspoons *each* chili powder and dried oregano

1 teaspoon *each* cumin seeds and crushed red pepper flakes

1 cup low-sodium chicken broth

1 pound ground turkey or chicken breast

1/2 cup cider vinegar

1 In a wide frying pan, combine onion, chili powder, oregano, cumin seeds, red pepper flakes, and broth. Bring to a boil over high heat; boil, stirring occasionally, until liquid has evaporated and browned bits stick to pan. Add 2 tablespoons water, stirring to scrape browned bits free; cook until mixture begins to brown again. Repeat this deglazing step, adding 2 tablespoons of water each time, until onion is a rich brown color.

2 Add 2 tablespoons more water, then crumble turkey into pan; cook, stirring, until browned bits stick to pan. Repeat deglazing step, adding vinegar in 2-tablespoon portions, until mixture is a rich brown color. If made ahead, let cool; then cover and refrigerate until next day.

makes about 3 1/2 cups

per serving: 48 calories, 8 g protein, 2 g carbohydrates, 0.5 g total fat, 20 mg cholesterol, 92 mg sodium

sautéed turkey with provolone & sage

preparation time: about 15 minutes

1 pound thinly sliced turkey breast

2 teaspoons finely chopped fresh sage or
  1 teaspoon dried sage

2 teaspoons olive oil

1/2 cup finely shredded provolone or part-skim
  mozzarella cheese

Pepper

Sage sprigs

Lemon wedges

Salt

1 Rinse turkey and pat dry. Sprinkle one side of each slice with chopped sage; set aside.

2 Heat 1 teaspoon of the oil in a wide nonstick frying pan over medium-high heat. Add half the turkey, sage-coated side down, and cook until golden on bottom (about 1 1/2 minutes). Then turn pieces over and continue to cook until no longer pink in center; cut to test (30 to 60 more seconds). Transfer cooked turkey to a platter and sprinkle with half the cheese. Cover loosely with foil and keep warm.

3 Repeat to cook remaining turkey; using remaining 1 teaspoon oil; add water, 1 tablespoon at a time, if pan appears dry. Transfer turkey to platter; sprinkle with remaining cheese.

4 Sprinkle turkey with pepper; garnish with sage sprigs. Season to taste with lemon and salt.

makes 4 servings

per serving: 184 calories, 31 g protein, 0.3 g carbohydrates, 6 g total fat, 78 mg cholesterol, 149 mg sodium

garlic chicken

preparation time: 15 minutes
cooking time: about 1 1/2 hours

1 large head garlic

1/2 teaspoon olive oil

4 boneless, skinless chicken breast halves
  (1 1/2 lbs. *total*)

1 tablespoon chopped fresh thyme or 1 teaspoon
  dried thyme

1/4 teaspoon coarsely ground pepper

1/8 teaspoon salt

1/2 cup shredded fontina cheese

4 small thyme sprigs

1 Slice 1/2 inch off top of garlic head. Then rub garlic with oil. Wrap garlic in foil and bake in a 375° oven until very soft when pressed (about 1 1/4 hours). Carefully remove garlic from foil; transfer to a rack and let stand until cool enough to touch (about 10 minutes).

2 Meanwhile, rinse chicken, pat dry, and sprinkle with chopped thyme and pepper. Place, skinned side up, in a lightly oiled 9-inch baking pan. Bake in a 450° oven until meat in thickest part is no longer pink; cut to test (12 to 15 minutes). Meanwhile, squeeze garlic cloves from skins into a small bowl. Add salt; mash garlic thoroughly with a fork, incorporating salt.

3 Spread a fourth of the garlic mixture over each chicken piece; then sprinkle chicken with cheese. Return to oven; continue to bake just until cheese is melted and bubbly (about 3 more minutes). Press a thyme sprig into cheese on each piece of chicken.

makes 4 servings

per serving: 258 calories, 43 g protein, 9 g carbohydrates, 5 g total fat, 107 mg cholesterol, 241 mg sodium

chicken in a squash shell

preparation time: about 1 hour

Nonstick cooking spray

2 small acorn squash

Soy-Ginger Sauce (recipe follows)

1 tablespoon salad oil

1 pound boneless and skinless chicken breasts, cut into 1/2-inch cubes

1/2 cup *each* finely diced red bell pepper and jicama

1 small onion, finely chopped

2 small firm-ripe tomatoes, peeled and finely diced

1 teaspoon Szechuan peppercorns, coarsely ground, or 1/2 teaspoon pepper

1/4 cup chopped green onions (including tops)

Plain lowfat yogurt (optional)

1. Lightly coat a 9- by 13-inch baking pan with cooking spray. With a sharp, heavy knife, cut squash in half lengthwise and scoop out seeds. Arrange squash, cut sides down, in pan. Bake in a 400° oven until tender when pierced (about 40 minutes).

2. Meanwhile, prepare Soy-Ginger Sauce and set aside.

3. About 15 minutes before squash is done, heat oil in a wide frying pan or wok over medium-high heat. Add chicken and cook, stirring, until meat in center is no longer pink; cut to test (2 to 3 minutes). Lift out with a slotted spoon and set aside. Add bell pepper, jicama, onion, tomatoes, and peppercorns to pan; cook, stirring, for 5 minutes. Add sauce; boil until thickened. Return chicken and any juices to pan, remove from heat, and keep warm.

4. Place squash in individual bowls and fill with chicken mixture. Sprinkle with green onions. Offer with yogurt, if desired.

makes 4 servings

SOY-GINGER SAUCE

Stir together 2 tablespoons each reduced-sodium soy sauce and dry sherry, 3/4 cup low-sodium chicken broth, 1 tablespoon each cornstarch and firmly packed brown sugar, and 1 teaspoon finely minced fresh ginger.

per serving: 282 calories, 29 g protein, 30 g carbohydrates, 6 g total fat, 66 mg cholesterol, 396 mg sodium

chicken enchilada bake

preparation time: about 50 minutes

12 corn tortillas (7-inch diameter)

5 medium-size tomatoes, peeled and thinly sliced

2 cups skinless and boneless shredded cooked chicken breast

1 cup thinly sliced green onions (including tops)

1 tablespoon margarine

2 tablespoons all-purpose flour

2 cups low-sodium chicken broth

1 cup plain lowfat yogurt

1 can (4 oz.) diced green chiles

2 ounces (about 1/2 cup) grated Cheddar cheese

1. Dip tortillas, one at a time, in water; let drain briefly. Stack and cut into 8 wedges. Spread a third of the tortillas in a 9- by 13-inch baking pan. Top with half the tomatoes; cover with half the chicken and onions. Repeat layers, ending with tortillas. Set aside.

2. In a 2- to 3-quart pan, melt margarine over medium heat. Add flour and cook, stirring, for 20 seconds. Whisk in chicken broth and bring to a boil. Remove from heat and add yogurt and chiles, whisking until smooth. Pour over tortilla mixture.

3. Cover and bake in a 375° oven for 20 minutes. Remove cover, sprinkle with Cheddar, and continue baking, uncovered, until cheese is melted (about 10 more minutes).

makes 8 servings

per serving: 254 calories, 19 g protein, 28 g carbohydrates, 8 g total fat, 39 mg cholesterol, 293 mg sodium

curried turkey & coconut rice

preparation time: about 45 minutes

1 cup low-fat (1%) milk

1 cup long-grain white rice

¼ cup sweetened shredded coconut

2 tablespoons lemon juice

1 clove garlic, minced or pressed

½ teaspoon ground cumin

¼ teaspoon chili powder

2 turkey breast tenderloins (about 1 lb. *total*),
   cut into 1-inch pieces

½ cup golden raisins

¼ cup dry white wine

2 medium-size carrots, cut into ¼-inch slanting
   slices

1 large onion, thinly sliced

2 teaspoons olive oil or vegetable oil

2 to 3 teaspoons curry powder

1 to 2 tablespoons chopped fresh mint

2 tablespoons salted roasted cashews, chopped

Mint or parsley sprigs

1 To prepare coconut rice, in a 3- to 4-quart pan, combine 1 cup water and milk. Bring just to a boil over medium-high heat. Stir in rice. Reduce heat, cover, and simmer until liquid has been absorbed and rice is tender to bite (about 20 minutes). Stir in coconut. Keep warm until ready to serve, fluffing occasionally with a fork.

2 Meanwhile, in a large bowl, combine 1 tablespoon water, lemon juice, garlic, cumin, and chili powder. Add turkey and stir to coat. Set aside; stir occasionally. In a small bowl, combine raisins and wine; let stand until raisins are softened (about 10 minutes), stirring occasionally.

3 In a wide nonstick frying pan or wok, combine carrots, onion, and ¼ cup water. Cover and cook over medium-high heat until carrots are tender-crisp to bite (about 5 minutes). Uncover and stir-fry until liquid has evaporated. Remove vegetables from pan with a slotted spoon and keep warm.

4 Heat oil in pan. When oil is hot, add turkey mixture. Stir-fry just until meat is no longer pink in center; cut to test (3 to 4 minutes). Add water, 1 tablespoon at a time, if pan appears dry. Add curry powder and stir-fry just until fragrant (about 30 seconds; do not scorch).

5 Add raisins (and soaking liquid) to pan; return vegetables to pan. Bring to a boil; boil, stirring, until liquid has evaporated (about 2 minutes). Remove from heat; stir in chopped mint and cashews. Spoon coconut rice into 4 wide bowls; top with turkey mixture and garnish with mint sprigs.

makes 4 servings

per serving: 506 calories, 36 g protein, 70 g carbohydrates, 8 g total fat, 73 mg cholesterol, 156 mg sodium

BUYING AND STORING POULTRY: Fresh poultry should never be left at room temperature for long. If you buy your chicken and turkey at a supermarket, make it one of the last items you pick up; then get it home and into the refrigerator as quickly as possible. Cook fresh poultry within 3 days of purchase. If you can't use it that soon, enclose it securely in heavy-duty foil, freezer paper, or plastic bags, then freeze for up to 6 months.

turkey fajitas

preparation time: about 25 minutes

1/4 cup lime juice

1 tablespoon balsamic vinegar or red wine vinegar

1 clove garlic, minced or pressed

1/2 teaspoon ground coriander

1/2 teaspoon ground cumin

1/2 teaspoon honey

2 turkey breast tenderloins (about 1 lb. *total*), cut into 1/2- by 2-inch strips

4 reduced-fat flour tortillas (*each* 7 to 9 inches in diameter)

1 tablespoon olive oil

1 large green bell pepper, seeded and cut into thin strips

1 large red onion, thinly sliced

Lime wedges

1 In a large bowl, stir together lime juice, vinegar, garlic, coriander, cumin, and honey. Add turkey and stir to coat. Set aside to marinate, stirring occasionally.

2 Brush tortillas lightly with hot water; then stack tortillas, wrap in foil, and heat in a 350° oven until warm (10 to 12 minutes).

3 Meanwhile, heat 2 teaspoons of the oil in a wide nonstick frying pan or wok over medium-high heat. When oil is hot, add bell pepper and onion and stir-fry until vegetables are lightly browned (2 to 3 minutes). Remove vegetables from pan with a slotted spoon and keep warm.

4 Heat remaining 1 teaspoon oil in pan. When oil is hot, lift turkey from marinade and drain briefly (reserve marinade). Add turkey to pan and stir-fry until no longer pink in center; cut to test (2 to 3 minutes). Add marinade and bring to a boil; return vegetables to pan and mix gently. Spoon mixture onto a platter.

5 Offer tortillas and lime wedges alongside turkey mixture. Fill tortillas with turkey mixture; add a squeeze of lime, roll up, and eat out of hand.

makes 4 servings

per serving: 280 calories, 31 g protein, 23 g carbohydrates, 6 g total fat, 70 mg cholesterol, 356 mg sodium

turkey & mushroom burgers

preparation time: about 25 minutes

1 egg white

1/4 cup dry white wine

1/3 cup soft French bread crumbs

1/4 teaspoon salt

1/8 teaspoon pepper

1/4 cup finely chopped shallots

1 pound lean ground turkey breast

4 ounces mushrooms, finely chopped

Olive oil cooking spray

6 onion hamburger rolls, split and warmed

1 In a medium-size bowl, beat egg white and wine until blended. Stir in bread crumbs, salt, pepper, and shallots; then lightly mix in turkey and mushrooms. Shape turkey mixture into 6 patties, each about 1/2 inch thick.

2 Spray a wide nonstick frying pan with cooking spray. Place over medium-high heat; add turkey patties. Cook, turning once, until patties are lightly browned on both sides and juices run clear when a knife is inserted in center (8 to 10 minutes). Serve on warm rolls.

makes 6 servings

per serving: 235 calories, 24 g protein, 25 g carbohydrates, 3 g total fat, 47 mg cholesterol, 394 mg sodium

stuffed chicken breasts with chutney

preparation time: about 50 minutes

1 tablespoon olive oil

2 cloves garlic, minced or pressed

1 large onion, chopped

2 ¼ cups chopped spinach leaves

4 whole chicken breasts, skinned, boned, and split

1 tablespoon balsamic vinegar

½ cup low-sodium chicken broth

¼ cup chutney

1 Heat oil in a 12- to 14-inch frying pan over medium-high heat. Add garlic and onion and cook, stirring occasionally, until onion is soft (about 7 minutes). Add 2 cups of the spinach; let cool.

2 Rinse chicken; pat dry. Place each breast half between 2 sheets of plastic wrap. Pound with a flat-surfaced mallet to a thickness of about ¼ inch.

3 In center of each breast half, mound an equal portion of the spinach mixture. Roll meat around filling to enclose; fasten with wooden picks. Place chicken rolls in pan used for spinach.

4 In a small bowl, mix vinegar, broth, and chutney. Pour over chicken. Bring to a simmer over medium heat. Cover and simmer until meat is no longer pink and filling is hot in center; cut to test (about 8 minutes). Remove chicken from pan; remove wooden picks and keep chicken warm.

5 Increase heat to high and bring chutney mixture to a boil. Cook, stirring occasionally, until reduced to ½ cup (about 5 minutes); then pour over chicken. Garnish with remaining ¼ cup spinach.

makes 8 servings

per serving: 174 calories, 27g protein, 8 g carbohydrates, 3 g total fat, 66 mg cholesterol, 107 mg sodium

sherried chicken with onion marmalade

preparation time: about 35 minutes
marinating time: at least 30 minutes

6 small boneless, skinless chicken breast halves (1 ½ to 1 ¾ lbs. *total*)

3 tablespoons cream sherry

2 small red onions

½ cup dry red wine

1 tablespoon *each* red wine vinegar and honey

Italian or regular parsley sprigs

Salt and pepper

1 Rinse chicken, pat dry, and place in a heavy-duty plastic food-storage bag; add 2 tablespoons of the sherry. Seal bag and rotate to coat chicken with sherry Refrigerate for at least 30 minutes or up to 6 hours, turning bag over several times.

2 Thinly slice onions; wrap several slices airtight and refrigerate. In a wide frying pan, combine remaining onion slices, wine, vinegar, and honey. Cook over medium-high heat, stirring often, until liquid has evaporated. Remove from heat and stir in remaining 1 tablespoon sherry. Set aside.

3 Turn chicken and its marinade into a 9- by 13-inch baking pan; arrange chicken, skinned side up, in a single layer. Bake in a 450° oven until meat in thickest part is no longer pink; cut to test (12 to 15 minutes). With a slotted spoon, transfer chicken to a platter. Top with onion mixture. Garnish with reserved onion slices and parsley sprigs. Season to taste with salt and pepper.

makes 6 servings

per serving: 200 calories, 30 g protein, 9 g carbohydrates, 2 g total fat, 74 mg cholesterol, 91 mg sodium

mediterranean turkey with couscous

preparation time: about 25 minutes

2 turkey breast tenderloins (about 1 lb. *total*),
cut into 1/2-inch pieces

2 cloves garlic, minced or pressed

1 teaspoon paprika

1/2 teaspoon grated lemon peel

1/8 teaspoon salt (optional)

1/8 teaspoon pepper

2 teaspoons cornstarch

2 tablespoons balsamic vinegar

1 1/2 cups fat-free reduced-sodium chicken broth

2/3 cup low-fat (1%) milk

1 1/2 teaspoons chopped fresh oregano or
1/2 teaspoon dried oregano

1 cup couscous

1 medium-size red bell pepper, seeded and
cut into thin strips

2 teaspoons olive oil

1/3 to 1/2 cup chopped pitted calamata olives

1/4 cup finely chopped parsley

Oregano sprigs

1 In a large bowl, mix turkey, garlic, paprika, 1/4 teaspoon of the lemon peel, salt (if used), and pepper; set aside.

2 To prepare sauce, in a bowl, smoothly blend cornstarch and vinegar. Stir in 1/2 cup of the broth. Set aside.

3 In a 3- to 4-quart pan, combine remaining 1 cup broth, milk, chopped oregano, and remaining 1/4 teaspoon lemon peel. Bring just to a boil over medium-high heat; stir in couscous. Cover, remove from heat, and let stand until liquid has been absorbed (about 5 minutes). Transfer to a rimmed platter and keep warm; fluff occasionally with a fork.

4 While couscous is standing, in a wide nonstick frying pan or wok, combine bell pepper and 2 tablespoons water. Stir-fry over medium-high heat until pepper is just tender-crisp to bite (about 2 minutes); add water, 1 tablespoon at a time, if pan appears dry. Remove from pan with a slotted spoon and keep warm.

5 Heat oil in pan. When oil is hot, add turkey mixture and stir-fry just until meat is no longer pink in center; cut to test (2 to 3 minutes). Stir reserved sauce well; pour into pan. Then add bell pepper and olives; cook, stirring, until sauce boils and thickens slightly (1 to 2 minutes). Pour turkey mixture over couscous. Sprinkle with parsley and garnish with oregano sprigs.

makes 4 servings

per serving: 415 calories, 37 g protein, 44 g carbohydrates, 9 g total fat, 72 mg cholesterol, 823 mg sodium

CHECKING TO SEE IF YOUR CHICKEN IS DONE: For a whole chicken or turkey, insert a meat thermometer in thickest part of the thigh (not touching bone) after turning bird breast up. (For turkey breast, insert in thickest part, not touching bone.) Begin checking thermometer three-quarters of the way through cooking; when it registers the correct temperature (consult a temperature chart), the bird is done.

light cassoulet

preparation time: 30 minutes
cooking time: about 1 1/2 hours

1 large onion, chopped

2 medium-size carrots, thinly sliced

1 medium-size red bell pepper, seeded and thinly sliced

3 cloves garlic, minced or pressed

1 can (about 14 1/2 oz.) low-sodium stewed tomatoes

2/3 cups vegetable broth

2/3 cup dry red wine

1 teaspoon dried thyme

1 dried bay leaf

1/4 teaspoon *each* pepper and liquid hot pepper seasoning

2 cans (about 15 oz. *each*) cannellini (white kidney beans), drained and rinsed

1 1/2 pounds boneless, skinless chicken breasts, cut into 1-inch pieces

4 ounces turkey kielbasa (Polish sausage), thinly sliced

1/4 cup finely chopped parsley

1 In a 5- to 6-quart pan, combine onion, carrots, bell pepper, garlic, and 1/2 cup water. Cook over medium-high heat, stirring often, until liquid evaporates and browned bits stick to pan bottom (about 10 minutes). To deglaze pan, add 1/3 cup water, stirring to loosen browned bits from pan; continue to cook until browned bits form again. Repeat deglazing step about 2 more times or until vegetables are browned, using 1/3 cup water each time.

2 Stir in tomatoes and their liquid, broth, wine, thyme, bay leaf, pepper, and hot pepper seasoning. Bring to a boil; then reduce heat, cover, and simmer for 45 minutes.

3 Stir in beans; simmer, uncovered, for 10 minutes. Stir in chicken and sausage. Continue to simmer, uncovered, until chicken is no longer pink in center; cut to test (about 10 more minutes). Just before serving, remove and discard bay leaf. To serve, ladle mixture into bowls and sprinkle with parsley.

makes 8 servings

per serving: 240 calories, 29 g protein, 24 g carbohydrates, 3 g total fat, 59 mg cholesterol, 557 mg sodium

chicken jambalaya

preparation time: about 1 1/2 hours

1 tablespoon salad oil

1/2 pound Canadian bacon, diced

1 1/2 pounds skinned and boned chicken breasts, cut into bite-size chunks

1 large onion, chopped

3 cloves garlic, minced or pressed

2 large green bell peppers, seeded and chopped

1 cup chopped celery

6 large tomatoes, chopped

1 large can (15 oz.) no-salt-added tomato sauce

2 bay leaves, crumbled

1 teaspoon dry thyme leaves

2 teaspoons ground white pepper

1 teaspoon ground red pepper (cayenne)

1/2 cup chopped parsley

1 1/2 cups long-grain white rice

3 cups low-sodium chicken broth

1 Heat oil in a 12- to 14-inch frying pan over medium heat. Add Canadian bacon and chicken; cook, stirring often, until browned on all sides (about 6 minutes). Transfer chicken to a 4- to 5-quart casserole.

2 Add onion, garlic, bell peppers, and celery to pan. Cook, stirring occasionally, until onion is soft (about 10 minutes). Add tomatoes, tomato sauce, bay leaves, thyme, white pepper, red pepper, and parsley; cook, stirring occasionally, until sauce boils. Boil gently, uncovered, for 5 minutes.

3 Pour sauce over chicken; stir in rice and broth. Cover and bake in a 375° oven until rice is tender to bite (about 45 minutes).

makes 6 servings

per serving: 471 calories, 42 g protein, 57 g carbohydrates, 8 g total fat, 85 mg cholesterol, 685 mg sodium

apricot-mustard chicken

preparation time: about 30 minutes

1 can (12 oz.) apricot nectar

3 tablespoons Dijon mustard

3 whole chicken breasts (about 1 lb. *each*), skinned, boned, and split

2 1/2 cups low-sodium chicken broth

10 ounces (about 1 3/4 cups) couscous

2 tablespoons minced fresh basil leaves

Basil sprigs and lime wedges (optional)

1 In a wide frying pan, combine apricot nectar and mustard. Bring to a boil over high heat. Arrange chicken breasts, skinned sides down, in pan. Reduce heat, cover, and simmer for 10 minutes. Turn chicken and continue cooking until meat in thickest part is no longer pink; cut to test (5 to 8 more minutes).

2 Meanwhile, bring chicken broth to a boil in a 2- to 3-quart pan over high heat; stir in couscous. Cover, remove from heat, and let stand until broth is completely absorbed (about 5 minutes).

3 With a fork, fluff couscous; transfer to a platter. Lift out chicken with a slotted spoon and arrange over couscous; keep warm.

4 Boil apricot mixture over high heat, stirring often, until reduced to 1 cup (about 5 minutes). Pour over chicken and sprinkle with minced basil. Garnish with basil sprigs and lime, if desired.

makes 6 servings

per serving: 380 calories, 41 g protein, 46 g carbohydrates, 3 g total fat, 86 mg cholesterol, 352 mg sodium

turkey curry with soba

preparation time: about 50 minutes

1 tablespoon salad oil

1 pound boneless, skinless turkey breast, cut into
1 1/2-inch chunks

1 large onion, thinly sliced

1 clove garlic, minced or pressed

1 tablespoon grated fresh ginger

1 teaspoon *each* crushed red pepper flakes,
ground coriander, ground cumin, and
ground turmeric

1/2 teaspoon fennel seeds

1 cup low-sodium chicken broth

1 package (about 7 oz.) dry soba noodles

1 cup plain nonfat yogurt

1/4 cup unsalted dry-roasted cashews

1 Heat oil in a wide frying pan over medium heat. Add turkey and cook, stirring often, until browned on all sides (about 6 minutes). Using a slotted spoon, remove turkey from pan.

2 Add onion and garlic to pan; cook, stirring occasionally, until onion is soft (about 10 minutes). Add ginger, red pepper flakes, coriander, cumin, turmeric, and fennel seeds; cook, stirring, for 1 minute.

3 Return turkey to pan. Add broth and bring to a boil. Then reduce heat, cover, and simmer until meat is no longer pink in center; cut to test (about 20 minutes). Remove from heat.

4 While turkey is simmering, cook noodles in boiling water according to package directions until just tender to bite; drain well and pour into a large, shallow serving bowl.

5 Stir yogurt into turkey mixture, then pour mixture over noodles. Sprinkle with cashews.

makes 6 servings

per serving: 294 calories, 6 g total fat, 34 g carbohydrates, 27 g protein, 48 mg cholesterol, 340 mg sodium

turkey & lima bean stew

preparation time: about 20 minutes
cooking time: about 1 hour

1 large onion, chopped

2 cups sliced mushrooms

1 cup thinly sliced carrots

1 teaspoon dry thyme

3 cups low-sodium chicken broth

2 tablespoons lemon juice

2 pounds boneless, skinless turkey or chicken
thighs, trimmed of fat and cut into 1-inch chunks

1 tablespoon cornstarch

1 package (about 10 oz.) frozen baby lima beans,
thawed

1 In a 5- to 6-quart pan, combine onion, mushrooms, carrots, thyme, and 1 cup of the broth. Bring to a boil over high heat; then boil, stirring occasionally, until liquid evaporates and vegetables begin to brown (about 10 minutes). To deglaze, add 1/4 cup more broth and stir to scrape browned bits free. Then continue to cook, stirring occasionally, until vegetables begin to brown again. Repeat deglazing and browning steps, using 1/4 cup more broth each time, until vegetable mixture is richly browned. Then deglaze one last time with lemon juice.

2 Stir turkey and 1/2 cup more broth into vegetable mixture. Bring to a boil over high heat. Then reduce heat to low, cover, and simmer until turkey chunks are no longer pink in center; cut to test (about 40 minutes; about 25 minutes for chicken). Skim and discard fat from sauce.

3 Smoothly blend cornstarch with 3/4 cup of the broth. Add cornstarch mixture and beans to pan; bring to a boil over medium-high heat, stirring. Continue to boil, stirring, until beans are tender to bite.

makes 6 servings

per serving: 299 calories, 36 g protein, 20 g carbohydrates, 7 g total fat, 114 mg cholesterol, 182 mg sodium

kung pao chicken

preparation time: about 50 minutes

1 cup long-grain white rice

Cooking Sauce (recipe follows)

1 1/2 cups Chinese pea pods (also called snow or sugar peas) or sugar snap peas, ends and strings removed

1 tablespoon cornstarch

1 tablespoon dry white wine

1/2 teaspoon sugar

1 pound boneless, skinless chicken breast, cut into 3/4-inch chunks

2 cloves garlic, minced or pressed

1 cup peeled, shredded jicama

2 tablespoons salted roasted peanuts, chopped

1 In a 3- to 4-quart pan, bring 2 cups water to a boil over high heat; stir in rice. Reduce heat, cover, and simmer until liquid has been absorbed and rice is tender to bite (about 20 minutes). Meanwhile, prepare Cooking Sauce; set aside. Cut pea pods diagonally into 3/4-inch pieces; set aside.

2 In a large bowl, dissolve cornstarch in wine; stir in sugar. Add chicken and stir to coat. Then turn chicken mixture into a wide nonstick frying pan or wok; add garlic and 1 tablespoon water. Stir-fry over medium-high heat until meat is no longer pink in center; cut to test (4 to 6 minutes). Remove from pan with a slotted spoon and keep warm.

3 Add pea pods, jicama, and 1 tablespoon water to pan; stir-fry until pea pods are tender-crisp to bite (about 1 minute). Stir Cooking Sauce well; pour into pan and bring to a boil. Remove from heat and stir in chicken.

4 Spoon rice onto a rimmed platter; top with chicken mixture and sprinkle with peanuts.

makes 4 servings

COOKING SAUCE

Mix 1 tablespoon each sugar and chili paste with garlic; 1 tablespoon unseasoned rice vinegar or distilled white vinegar; and 1 tablespoon *each* hoisin sauce and Asian sesame oil.

per serving: 425 calories, 33 g protein, 51 g carbohydrates, 9 g total fat, 66 mg cholesterol, 122 mg sodium

lemon turkey scaloppine

preparation time: about 25 minutes

1 pound skinned and boned turkey breast, sliced 1/2 inch thick

2 tablespoons all-purpose flour

1 tablespoon salad oil

1/2 cup lemon juice

2 tablespoons drained capers

1 lemon, thinly sliced

1 Rinse turkey, pat dry, and cut into serving-size pieces. Place between sheets of plastic wrap. With a flat-surfaced mallet, pound turkey to a thickness of about 1/4 inch. Dust with flour.

2 Heat oil in a 12- to 14-inch frying pan over medium-high heat. Add turkey and cook, turning once, until golden brown on both sides (about 4 minutes). With a slotted spoon, transfer turkey to a platter; keep warm.

3 Add lemon juice and capers to pan. Bring to a boil and cook, stirring, until thickened (about 2 minutes). Pour sauce over turkey; garnish with lemon slices.

makes 4 servings

per serving: 186 calories, 27 g protein, 8 g carbohydrates, 5 g total fat, 70 mg cholesterol, 193 mg sodium

grilled turkey with peaches

preparation time: about 30 minutes
grilling time: about 1 hour

1 teaspoon minced fresh ginger

²/₃ cup peach chutney or Major Grey's chutney

1 turkey breast half (about 3 lbs.), boned and skinned

3 large firm-ripe peaches; or 6 canned peach halves, drained

2 tablespoons lemon juice (if using fresh peaches)

6 green onions

1 At least 30 minutes before cooking, prepare a barbecue for indirect grilling.

2 In a blender or food processor, combine ginger and ⅓ cup of the chutney. Whirl until puréed. Coarsely chop remaining ⅓ cup chutney and set aside. Rinse turkey, pat dry, and brush all over with some of the chutney-ginger mixture.

3 Place turkey on grill directly above drip pan. Cover barbecue and open vents. Cook turkey, brushing occasionally with chutney mixture, until a meat thermometer inserted in thickest part registers 165° (about 1 hour).

4 Meanwhile, immerse fresh peaches in boiling water for 30 seconds; lift out and let cool for 1 minute. Peel, halve, and pit; coat with lemon juice. Peel off outer layer of onions; trim tops, leaving about 4 inches of green leaves.

5 About 10 minutes before turkey is done, lay peach halves (cut side down) and onions on grill directly above coals. Cook, turning once and brushing several times with chutney mixture, until peaches are hot and onion tops are wilted (about 10 minutes).

6 To serve, thinly slice turkey across the grain. Arrange on a platter and surround with peaches and onions. Offer reserved chopped chutney to add to taste.

makes 6 servings

per serving: 324 calories, 45 g protein, 31 g carbohydrates, 1 g total fat, 111 mg cholesterol, 406 mg sodium

layered turkey enchiladas

preparation time: about 15 minutes
baking time: about 1 hour and 20 minutes

1 cup shredded extra-sharp Cheddar cheese

1 pound ground skinned turkey breast

1 large can (7 oz.) diced green chiles

1 medium-size onion, chopped

1 cup mild green salsa

1 ½ cups chopped pear-shaped (Roma-type) tomatoes

8 corn tortillas (*each* 6 to 7 inches in diameter)

1 Mix ¾ cup of the cheese with turkey, chiles, onion, ½ cup of the salsa, and 1 cup of the tomatoes. Divide into 7 equal portions.

2 Place 1 tortilla in a shallow 9- to 10-inch diameter baking pan; cover evenly with one portion of the turkey mixture. Repeat to use remaining tortillas and turkey mixture; top stack with a tortilla. Cover with remaining ¼ cup cheese, ½ cup salsa, and ½ cup tomatoes.

3 Cover with foil and bake in a 400° oven for 40 minutes. Uncover and continue to bake until turkey is no longer pink; cut to center of stack to test (about 40 more minutes). Let stand for 5 minutes, then cut into wedges.

makes 4 to 6 servings

per serving: 284 calories, 26 g protein, 25 g carbohydrates, 9 g total fat, 67 mg cholesterol, 684 mg sodium

arroz con pollo

preparation time: about 15 minutes
cooking time: about 1 hour and 10 minutes

1 can (about 14 ¹/₂ oz.) tomatoes

About 1 ¹/₂ cups low-sodium chicken broth

1 chicken (3 to 3 ¹/₂ lbs.), cut up and skinned

1 teaspoon salad oil

1 large onion, chopped

1 small green pepper, seeded and chopped

2 cloves garlic, minced or pressed (optional)

1 cup long-grain white rice

1 teaspoon dry oregano

¹/₄ teaspoon *each* ground cumin and pepper

1 dry bay leaf

1 package (about 10 oz.) frozen tiny peas, thawed

Salt

¹/₄ cup thinly sliced green onions

1 Drain liquid from tomatoes into a glass measure; add enough broth to make 2 cups liquid.

2 Rinse chicken and pat dry. Heat oil in a 4- to 5-quart pan over medium-high heat. Add several pieces of chicken (do not crowd pan) and 2 tablespoons water; cook, turning as needed, until chicken is browned on all sides (about 10 minutes). Add more water, 1 tablespoon at a time, if pan appears dry. Repeat to brown remaining chicken, setting pieces aside as they are browned. Discard all but 1 teaspoon of the drippings.

3 Add chopped onion, bell pepper, and garlic (if desired) to pan; cook, stirring, until onion is soft (about 5 minutes). Stir in tomatoes (break them up with a spoon), broth mixture, rice, oregano, cumin, pepper, and bay leaf. Bring to a boil.

4 Return chicken to pan. Reduce heat, cover, and simmer until meat near thighbone is no longer pink; cut to test (about 45 minutes). Add more broth as needed to prevent sticking. Stir in peas; season to taste with salt. Just before serving, garnish with green onions.

makes 6 servings

per serving: 331 calories, 32 g protein, 38 g carbohydrates, 6 g total fat, 83 mg cholesterol, 299 mg sodium

devilishly spicy chicken

preparation time: about 15 minutes
cooking time: about 1 hour

1 chicken (about 4 lbs.), cut up and skinned

2 tablespoons butter or margarine

2 medium-size onions, chopped

1 tablespoon dry mustard

1 can or bottle (about 12 oz.) beer

¹/₃ cup tomato-based chili sauce

3 tablespoons Worcestershire

4 cups hot cooked eggless noodles

1 package (about 10 oz.) frozen tiny peas, thawed

1 Rinse chicken, pat dry, and set aside.

2 Melt butter in a wide frying pan over medium-high heat. Add onions; cook, stirring often, until golden brown (12 to 15 minutes). Stir in mustard, beer, chili sauce, and Worcestershire. Add all chicken pieces except breasts; turn to coat. Reduce heat, cover, and simmer for 20 minutes. Turn chicken over. Add breasts to pan, cover, and continue to simmer until meat near thighbone is no longer pink; cut to test (about 20 more minutes).

3 Spoon noodles onto a deep platter. Lift chicken from pan and arrange over noodles; keep warm. Bring cooking liquid to a boil; boil, uncovered, stirring often, until reduced to 2 cups (6 to 8 minutes). Add peas and stir until heated through. Spoon sauce over chicken.

makes 4 to 6 servings

per serving: 461 calories, 46 g protein, 43 g carbohydrates, 11 g total fat, 134 mg cholesterol, 610 mg sodium

creamy barley with chicken

preparation time: 15 minutes
cooking time: about 40 minutes

2 teaspoons olive oil

2 boneless, skinless chicken breast halves (about 12 oz. *total*), cut into $^3/_4$-inch pieces

$^1/_4$ teaspoon salt (or to taste)

1 large onion, chopped

1 $^1/_2$ teaspoons chopped fresh sage or $^3/_4$ teaspoon dried rubbed sage

$^1/_4$ teaspoon pepper

3 $^1/_2$ cups vegetable broth

1 $^1/_3$ cups pearl barley, rinsed and drained

1 package (about 10 oz.) frozen corn kernels, thawed and drained

1 can (about 15 oz.) cream-style corn

$^1/_4$ cup finely chopped parsley

Sage sprigs (optional)

1 Heat oil in a 4- to 5-quart pan over medium-high heat. Add chicken and salt. Cook, stirring often, until chicken is no longer pink in center; cut to test (2 to 3 minutes). Remove from pan with a slotted spoon and set aside.

2 Add onion, chopped sage, pepper, and $^1/_4$ cup water to pan. Cook, stirring often, until onion is soft (about 5 minutes). Stir in broth and barley and bring to a boil; then reduce heat, cover, and simmer until barley is tender to bite (about 30 minutes).

3 Add corn kernels, cream-style corn, and chicken. Cook, stirring, just until heated through. Spoon barley mixture onto a rimmed platter and sprinkle with parsley. Garnish with sage sprigs, if desired.

makes 6 servings

per serving: 352 calories, 21 g protein, 62 g carbohydrates, 4 g total fat, 33 mg cholesterol, 874 mg sodium

chicken breasts with blueberries

preparation time: about 35 minutes

4 boneless, skinless chicken breast halves (about 1 $^1/_2$ lbs. *total*)

1 tablespoon salad oil

$^1/_2$ cup apricot jam

3 tablespoons Dijon mustard

$^1/_2$ cup frozen unsweetened blueberries

$^1/_3$ cup white wine vinegar

Watercress sprigs

1 Rinse chicken and pat dry. Heat oil in a wide frying pan over medium-high heat. Add chicken; cook, turning as needed, until browned on both sides (about 6 minutes).

2 Meanwhile, in a small bowl, stir together jam and mustard. Spread jam mixture over tops of chicken pieces; sprinkle with blueberries. Reduce heat to medium-low, cover, and cook until meat in thickest part is no longer pink; cut to test (about 15 minutes). With a slotted spoon, lift chicken and blueberries to a platter. Keep warm.

3 Add vinegar to pan, increase heat to high, and bring sauce to a boil. Then boil, uncovered, stirring occasionally, until sauce is reduced by about a third (about 5 minutes). Pour sauce evenly over chicken; garnish with watercress sprigs.

makes 4 servings

per serving: 340 calories, 40 g protein, 30 g carbohydrates, 6 g total fat, 99 mg cholesterol, 464 mg sodium

stuffed chicken legs with capellini

preparation time: about 1 1/2 hours

1/2 cup *each* cilantro leaves and fresh basil

1/2 cup freshly grated Parmesan cheese

3 whole chicken legs (about 1 1/2 lbs. *total*)

3 large red bell peppers

4 slices bacon

12 ounces dried capellini

1/2 cup seasoned rice vinegar; or 1/2 cup distilled white vinegar and 4 teaspoons sugar

1/4 cup capers, drained

1 tablespoon grated lemon peel

Finely shredded lemon peel

Cilantro sprigs

Salt and pepper

1 Combine cilantro leaves, basil, and cheese in a food processor or blender. Whirl until minced.

2 Cut a slit just through skin at joint on outside of each chicken leg. Slide your fingers between skin and meat to separate, leaving skin in place. Tuck cilantro mixture under skin, spreading evenly. Set aside.

3 Place bell peppers on a lightly greased grill 4 to 6 inches above a solid bed of hot coals. Grill, turning as needed, until charred all over (about 10 minutes). Cover with foil and let cool. Pull off and discard skin, stems, and seeds. Cut into strips and set aside.

4 Lay chicken on grill when coals have cooled down to medium heat and cook, turning as needed, until meat near thighbone is no longer pink; cut to test (about 40 minutes). Meanwhile, cook bacon in a wide nonstick frying pan over medium heat until crisp (about 5 minutes). Lift out, drain well, and crumble; set aside. Discard all but 2 teaspoons of the drippings; set pan with drippings aside.

5 Bring 12 cups water to a boil in a 5- to 6-quart pan over medium-high heat. Stir in pasta and cook just until tender to bite (about 4 minutes); or cook according to package directions. Drain well and keep warm.

6 Add vinegar, capers, and grated lemon peel to pan with drippings. Bring just to a boil over medium heat. Add pasta and bacon. Cook, stirring, just until warm. Transfer to a platter. Cut chicken legs apart. Place chicken and bell peppers on platter. Garnish with shredded lemon peel and cilantro sprigs. Offer salt and pepper to add to taste.

makes 6 servings

per serving: 457 calories , 28 g protein, 52 g carbohydrates, 15 g total fat, 64 mg cholesterol, 858 mg sodium

shredded chicken filling

preparation time: about 1 hour

6 dried ancho or pasilla chiles

1 teaspoon salad oil

2 large onions, chopped

2 cloves garlic, minced or pressed

1 can (about 14 ¹/₂ oz.) tomatoes

2 teaspoons sugar

1 teaspoon dried oregano

¹/₂ teaspoon ground cumin

2 cups finely shredded cooked chicken or turkey breast

Salt and pepper

1 Place chiles on a baking sheet and toast in a 300° oven until fragrant (3 to 4 minutes). Remove from oven; let cool. Discard stems, seeds, and veins; then place chiles in a bowl, cover with 1 ¹/₂ cups boiling water, and let stand until pliable (about 30 minutes).

2 While chiles are soaking, place oil, onions, garlic, and 1 tablespoon water in a wide nonstick frying pan. Cook over medium heat, stirring often, until mixture is deep golden (20 to 30 minutes); if onions stick to pan or pan appears dry, add more water, 1 tablespoon at a time.

3 Drain chiles, discarding liquid. In a blender or food processor, whirl chiles, tomatoes and their liquid, sugar, oregano, and cumin until smoothly puréed.

4 Stir chicken and chile-tomato mixture into onion mixture. Reduce heat and simmer, uncovered, stirring occasionally, until mixture is thick and flavors are blended (about 10 minutes). Season to taste with salt and pepper.

makes about 3 cups

per serving: 90 calories, 9 g protein, 10 g carbohydrates, 3 g total fat, 20 mg cholesterol, 75 mg sodium

mu shu sandwiches

preparation time: about 20 minutes

1 tablespoon salad oil

3 cups thinly sliced onions

2 cups thinly sliced green or red bell peppers

1 pound boneless, skinless chicken breast, cut into ¹/₂- by 2-inch strips

¹/₄ cup hoisin sauce

Whole green onions (ends trimmed)

4 pita breads (*each* about 6 inches in diameter), cut crosswise into halves

Pickled scallions and pickled sliced ginger (optional)

1 Heat 2 teaspoons of the oil in a wide nonstick frying pan or wok over medium-high heat. When oil is hot, add onions and peppers; stir-fry until vegetables are lightly browned (2 to 3 minutes). Remove from pan with a slotted spoon; keep warm.

2 Heat remaining 1 teaspoon oil in pan. When oil is hot, add chicken and stir-fry until no longer pink in center; cut to test (3 to 4 minutes). Add hoisin sauce to pan; then return vegetables to pan and stir to mix well.

3 Pour into a bowl and garnish with green onions. Fill bread halves with chicken mixture and, if desired, pickled scallions and pickled ginger.

makes 4 servings

per serving: 379 calories, 33 g protein, 45 g carbohydrates, 6 g total fat, 66 mg cholesterol, 400 mg sodium

summer turkey stir-fry

preparation time: about 30 minutes

Cooking Sauce (recipe follows)

1 ³/₄ cups water

1 cup bulgur

1 tablespoon salad oil

3 cloves garlic, minced or pressed

1 pound boneless, skinless turkey breast, cut into ³/₄-inch chunks

3 cups thinly sliced carrots

2 small zucchini, sliced

2 tablespoons minced fresh ginger

¹/₂ cup thinly sliced green onions

1 Prepare Cooking Sauce and set aside.

2 In a 2- to 3-quart pan, bring 1 ¹/₂ cups of the water to a boil over high heat; stir in bulgur. Reduce heat, cover, and simmer until bulgur is tender to bite and water has been absorbed (about 15 minutes).

3 Meanwhile, heat oil in a wide frying pan or wok over high heat. Add garlic and turkey and cook, stirring, until meat is no longer pink in center; cut to test (about 5 minutes). Add carrots, zucchini, ginger, and remaining ¹/₄ cup water. Cover and continue to cook, stirring occasionally, until vegetables are tender-crisp to bite (about 5 more minutes). Uncover, bring to a boil, and boil until almost all liquid has evaporated. Stir in Cooking Sauce; boil, stirring, until sauce is bubbly and thickened.

4 To serve, spoon bulgur onto individual plates and top with turkey mixture. Sprinkle with onions.

makes 4 servings

COOKING SAUCE

In a small bowl, mix ¹/₂ cup low-sodium chicken broth, 2 tablespoons reduced-sodium soy sauce, and 1 tablespoon cornstarch.

per serving: 345 calories, 35 g protein, 41 g carbohydrates, 5 g total fat, 70 mg cholesterol, 402 mg sodium

apricot-stuffed turkey roast

preparation time: about 15 minutes
roasting time: about 1 ¹/₄ hours

1 turkey breast half (about 3 ¹/₂ lbs.), boned and skinned

3 tablespoons Dijon mustard

1 teaspoon dry rosemary

10 to 12 dried apricots

1 tablespoon olive oil

1 teaspoon minced or pressed garlic

Pepper

1 Rinse turkey and pat dry; then place, skinned side down, on a board. Make a lengthwise cut down center of thickest part of turkey, being careful not to cut all the way through. Push cut open and press meat to make it lie as flat as possible.

2 Spread turkey with mustard and sprinkle with ¹/₂ teaspoon of the rosemary; then top evenly with apricots. Starting at a long edge, roll up turkey firmly jelly roll style, enclosing filling. Tie roll snugly with cotton string at 2- to 3-inch intervals. Rub turkey with oil, then garlic; pat remaining ¹/₂ teaspoon rosemary over turkey and sprinkle generously with pepper.

3 Place turkey on a rack in a 9- by 13-inch baking pan. Roast in a 375° oven until a meat thermometer inserted in thickest part registers 165° and meat in center is no longer pink; cut to test (1 hour and 15 to 20 minutes). Let stand for about 10 minutes; then remove strings and cut roll crosswise into thick slices.

makes 6 to 8 servings

per serving: 238 calories, 44 g protein, 4 g carbohydrates, 4 g total fat, 111 mg cholesterol, 282 mg sodium

roast turkey with apple orzo

preparation time: about 20 minutes
cooking time: about 2 1/4 hours

2 tablespoons chopped pecans

1 boned turkey breast half (3 to 3 1/2 lbs.), trimmed of fat

1/3 cup apple jelly

1 tablespoon raspberry vinegar or red wine vinegar

1/4 teaspoon ground sage

2 cups apple juice

about 2 3/4 cups low-sodium chicken broth

10 ounces (about 1 2/3 cups) dried orzo or other rice-shaped pasta

1/2 cup dried cranberries or raisins

1/4 teaspoon ground coriander

1 tablespoon cornstarch mixed with 3 tablespoons cold water

1/3 cup chopped parsley or green onions

Sage sprigs

Salt and pepper

1 Toast nuts in a small frying pan over medium heat, shaking pan often, until golden (about 4 minutes). Remove from pan and set aside.

2 Place turkey skin side up. Fold narrow end under breast; pull skin to cover as much breast as possible. Tie snugly lengthwise and crosswise with cotton string at 1-inch intervals. Place in a nonstick or lightly oiled square 8-inch pan.

3 Combine jelly, vinegar, and ground sage in a 1- to 1 1/2-quart pan. Cook over medium-low heat, stirring, until jelly is melted. Baste turkey with some of the mixture, reserving remaining mixture.

4 Roast turkey in a 375° oven, basting with pan drippings and remaining jelly mixture, until a meat thermometer inserted in thickest part registers 160° (about 2 hours); if drippings start to scorch, add 1/3 cup water to pan, stirring to loosen browned bits. Meanwhile, combine apple juice and 1 1/3 cups of the broth in a 4- to 5-quart pan. Bring to a boil over high heat. Stir in pasta, cranberries, and coriander. Reduce heat, cover, and simmer, stirring occasionally, until almost all liquid is absorbed (about 15 minutes); do not scorch. Remove from heat and keep warm, stirring occasionally.

5 Transfer turkey to a warm platter; cover and let stand for 10 minutes. Meanwhile, pour pan drippings and accumulated juices into a 2-cup glass measure; skim off and discard fat. Stir cornstarch mixture and blend into drippings. Add enough of the remaining broth to make 1 1/2 cups. Pour into a 1- to 1 1/2-quart pan and cook over medium-high heat, stirring, until boiling. Pour into a serving container.

6 Remove strings from turkey. Slice meat and arrange on individual plates. Stir parsley into pasta and mound beside turkey; sprinkle with nuts. Garnish with sage sprigs. Offer gravy, salt, and pepper to add to taste.

makes 8 to 10 servings

per serving: 456 calories, 41 g protein, 45 g carbohydrates, 12 g total fat, 93 mg cholesterol, 104 mg sodium

chicken chimichangas

preparation time: about 15 minutes
cooking time: about 40 minutes

Shredded Chicken Filling (page 222)

About 1 1/2 cups salsa of your choice

5 cups shredded lettuce

1 1/2 cups shredded carrots

8 flour tortillas (7- to 9-inch diameter)

About 1/3 cup nonfat milk

1/2 cup shredded Cheddar cheese

Plain nonfat yogurt

1 Prepare Shredded Chicken Filling; set aside. In a small bowl, mix lettuce and carrots; set aside.

2 To assemble each chimichanga, brush both sides of a tortilla liberally with milk; let stand briefly to soften tortilla. Spoon an eighth of the filling down the center of tortilla; top with 1 table-spoon of the cheese. Lap ends of tortilla over filling; then fold sides to center to make a packet. Place chimichanga, seam side down, on a lightly oiled 12- by 15-inch baking sheet and brush with milk. Repeat to make 7 more chimichangas.

3 Bake in a 500° oven, brushing with milk after 5 minutes, until golden brown (8 to 10 minutes).

4 To serve, divide lettuce mixture among 8 plates; place 1 chimichanga on each plate. Add salsa and yogurt to taste.

makes 8 servings

per serving: 291 calories, 19 g protein, 37 g carbohydrates, 9 g total fat, 38 mg cholesterol, 338 mg sodium

oregano-rubbed turkey

preparation time: about 20 minutes
marinating time: at least 2 hours

1 tablespoon salt

1 1/2 teaspoons sugar

1 1/2 pounds thinly sliced turkey breast

1/4 cup sliced green onions

2 tablespoons finely chopped Italian or regular parsley

3 cloves garlic, minced

1 teaspoon chopped fresh oregano or 1/2 teaspoon dried oregano

1/2 teaspoon *each* coarsely ground pepper and grated lemon peel

2 teaspoons olive oil

Italian or regular parsley sprigs

Lemon wedges

1 In a large bowl, combine salt and sugar. Rinse turkey and pat dry; then add to bowl and turn to coat evenly with salt mixture. Cover and refrigerate for at least 2 hours or up to 3 hours. Rinse turkey well, drain, and pat dry.

2 In a small bowl, combine onions, chopped parsley, garlic, oregano, pepper, and lemon peel. Rub onion mixture evenly over both sides of each turkey slice.

3 Heat 1 teaspoon of the oil in a wide nonstick frying pan over medium-high heat. Add half the turkey and cook until golden on bottom (about 1 1/2 minutes). Then turn pieces over and continue to cook until no longer pink in center; cut to test (30 to 60 more seconds). Transfer cooked turkey to a platter, cover loosely with foil, and keep warm.

4 Immediately cook remaining turkey, using remaining 1 teaspoon oil; add water, 1 tablespoon at a time, if pan appears dry. Transfer turkey to platter and garnish with parsley sprigs. Serve at once. Season to taste with lemon.

makes 6 servings

per serving: 148 calories, 28 g protein, 2 g carbohydrates, 2 g total fat, 70 mg cholesterol, 1,155 mg sodium

chili & anise chicken tortas

preparation time: about 35 minutes

1 pound skinless, bone less chicken thighs

4 cups water

2 cups low-sodium chicken broth

¼ cup chili powder

4 cup firmly packed brown sugar

2 teaspoons dried oregano

1 teaspoon anise seeds

About 1 tablespoon red wine vinegar, or to taste

2 tablespoons *each* chopped cilantro and thinly sliced green onion

4 French rolls (*each* about 6 inches long)

8 to 12 butter lettuce leaves, rinsed and crisped

CONDIMENTS:

Avocado slices and asadero or string cheese

1 Rinse chicken and pat dry; set aside. In a 4- to 5-quart pan with a tight-fitting lid, combine water, broth, chili powder, sugar, oregano, and anise seeds. Bring to a rolling boil over high heat. Remove pan from heat and immediately add chicken. Cover pan and let stand until meat in thickest part is no longer pink; cut to test (15 to 20 minutes; do not uncover until ready to test). If chicken is not done, return it to hot water, cover, and let steep for 2 to 3 more minutes.

2 Drain chicken, reserving 2 cups of the cooking liquid. Return reserved liquid to pan. Bring to a boil over high heat; boil until reduced to ½ cup, watching closely to prevent scorching.

3 Serve chicken and sauce warm or cold. To serve, stir vinegar, cilantro, and onion into sauce. Cut chicken across the grain into thin slanting slices; set aside. Cut rolls in half lengthwise and moisten cut surfaces evenly with sauce. Fill rolls with chicken and lettuce. Offer additional sauce and condiments to add to taste.

makes 4 servings

per serving: 464 calories, 33 g protein, 68 g carbohydrates, 7 g total fat, 94 mg cholesterol, 1,819 mg sodium

brunch paella

preparation time: about 55 minutes

1 pound turkey Italian sausages (casings removed), crumbled into ½-inch pieces

1 cup long-grain white rice

1 large onion (about 8 oz.), chopped

2 cloves garlic, minced or pressed

2 cups fat-free reduced sodium chicken broth

1 ½ cups chopped tomatoes

¼ teaspoon saffron threads

1 package (about 9 oz.) frozen artichoke hearts, thawed and drained

¼ cup chopped parsley

Lemon wedges

1 In a wide nonstick frying pan or wok, stir-fry sausage over medium-high heat until browned (7 to 10 minutes). Remove sausage from pan with a slotted spoon; set aside. Pour off and discard all but 1 teaspoon fat from pan.

2 Add rice to pan; stir-fry until rice begins to torn opaque (about 3 minutes). Add onion, garlic, and 2 tablespoons water; stir-fry for 5 more minutes. Add more water, 1 tablespoon at a time, if pan appears dry.

3 Stir in broth, tomatoes, saffron, artichokes, and parsley; then return sausage to pan. Bring to a boil; reduce heat, cover, and simmer until liquid has been absorbed and rice is tender to bite (about 20 minutes). Serve with lemon wedges.

makes 4 to 6 servings

per serving: 195 calories, 7 g protein, 41 g carbohydrates, 0.7 g total fat, 0 mg cholesterol, 294 mg sodium

yucatan tamale pie

preparation time: about 1 ½ hours

**3 ounces achiote condiment or substitute
(recipe follows)**

2 cups low-sodium chicken broth

**2 tablespoons minced fresh mint or 1 teaspoon
dry mint**

¹⁄₈ teaspoon anise seeds

3 cups bite-size pieces of cooked chicken

2 large onions, chopped

2 large tomatoes, cored and cut into wedges

**2 tablespoons cornstarch mixed with ¹⁄₄ cup
cold water**

Masa Topping (recipe follows)

Cilantro sprigs

1 Place achiote condiment (or substitute) in a 2-quart pan; stir in ½ cup of the broth. With a heavy spoon, work mixture into a smooth paste. Stir in remaining 1 ½ cups broth, mint, and anise seeds. Bring to a boil over high heat. Then reduce heat and simmer, uncovered, for 5 minutes, stirring often to prevent sticking. (At this point, you may let cool, then cover and refrigerate until next day.)

2 Stir chicken, onions, tomatoes, and cornstarch mixture into achiote mixture; pour into a deep 2- to 3-quart casserole and spread evenly. Prepare Masa Topping; drop in spoonfuls over chicken mixture.

3 Bake on bottom rack of a 400° oven until filling is bubbly in center and topping is well browned (about 45 minutes). Remove from oven and let stand for 5 minutes before serving. Garnish with cilantro sprigs.

makes 6 servings

ACHIOTE SUBSTITUTE

In a small bowl, mix 3 tablespoons paprika, 2 tablespoons distilled white vinegar, 1 ½ teaspoons dry oregano, 3 cloves garlic (minced), and ½ teaspoon ground cumin.

MASA TOPPING

In a small bowl, combine ½ cup each masa harina (dehydrated masa flour) and all-purpose flour. Stir in 1½ teaspoons baking powder. Add 1 large egg white, 1½ tablespoons salad oil, and ½ cup nonfat milk; stir just until blended.

per serving: 316 calories, 26 g protein, 30 g carbohydrates, 10 g total fat, 63 mg cholesterol, 215 mg sodium

honeyed chicken

preparation time: about 30 minutes

2 tablespoons sesame seeds

3 tablespoons honey

¹⁄₄ cup *each* dry sherry and Dijon mustard

1 tablespoon lemon juice

**3 whole chicken breasts (about 1 lb. *each*),
skinned, boned, and split**

1 In a small frying pan, toast sesame seeds over medium heat, shaking pan often, until golden (about 3 minutes). Transfer to a small bowl and add honey, sherry, mustard, and lemon juice; stir until blended.

2 Arrange chicken breasts, slightly apart, in a 9- by 13-inch baking pan. Drizzle with honey mixture. Bake in a 400° oven, basting several times with sauce, until meat in thickest part is no longer pink; cut to test (15 to 20 minutes). Transfer chicken to individual plates. Offer with any remaining sauce.

makes 6 servings

per serving: 229 calories, 35 g protein, 12 g carbohydrates, 4 g total fat, 86 mg cholesterol, 398 mg sodium

chicken-yogurt enchilada casserole

preparation time: about 1 hour

1 cup plain nonfat yogurt

1 cup low-fat (1%) cottage cheese

2 cloves garlic, peeled

2 teaspoons *each* chili powder, sugar, and cornstarch

1 tablespoon butter or margarine

1/4 cup all-purpose flour

2 cups low-sodium chicken broth

1 large can (about 7 oz.) diced green chiles

12 corn tortillas (6-inch diameter)

2 cups bite-size pieces of cooked chicken

1 small onion, chopped

1/2 cup shredded jack cheese

1 In a blender or food processor, whirl yogurt, cottage cheese, garlic, chili powder, sugar, and cornstarch until smoothly puréed. Set aside.

2 Melt butter in a 1 1/2- to 2-quart pan over medium-high heat. Add flour and 1/3 cup water; stir just until bubbly. Whisk in broth; bring to a boil, stirring. Remove from heat; let cool for 5 minutes. Whisk yogurt mixture into flour mixture; stir in chiles. Cover bottom of a 9- by 13-inch baking dish with a third of the yogurt-flour mixture.

3 Dip tortillas, one at a time, in hot water. Drain briefly; cut into strips 1 inch wide. Scatter half the tortilla strips over yogurt-flour mixture in baking dish; cover with all the chicken and onion, half the jack cheese, and half the remaining yogurt-flour mixture. Top with remaining tortilla strips, yogurt-flour mixture, and jack cheese.

4 Cover dish tightly with foil and bake in a 400° oven for 30 minutes. Uncover; continue to bake until mixture is golden brown on top and appears firm in center when dish is gently shaken (15 to 20 more minutes).

makes 8 servings

per serving: 261 calories, 20 g protein, 29 g carbohydrates, 8 g total fat, 41 mg cholesterol, 465 mg sodium

oven fried chicken

preparation time: about 35 minutes
marinating time: 20 minutes

2 tablespoons dry sherry

2 cloves garlic, minced or pressed

4 boneless, skinless chicken breast halves (about 1 1/2 lbs. *total*)

1/2 cup soft whole wheat bread crumbs

2 tablespoons cornmeal

1 teaspoon paprika

1/2 teaspoon *each* salt, pepper, dry sage, dry thyme, and dry basil

Vegetable oil cooking spray

1 In a shallow bowl, stir together sherry and garlic. Rinse chicken and pat dry; add to sherry mixture, turn to coat, and let stand for 20 minutes.

2 In another shallow bowl, mix bread crumbs, cornmeal, paprika, salt, pepper, sage, thyme, and basil. Lift chicken from marinade and drain briefly; discard marinade. Turn each chicken piece in crumb mixture to coat.

3 Lightly coat a shallow baking pan with cooking spray; arrange chicken pieces in pan. Bake in a 450° oven until meat in thickest part is no longer pink; cut to test (15 to 20 minutes). Serve hot or cold.

makes 4 servings

per serving: 231 calories, 40 g protein, 8 g, carbohydrates, 3 g total fat, 99 mg cholesterol, 418 mg sodium

stir-fried turkey with coconut rice

preparation time: about 45 minutes

Coconut Rice (recipe follows)

2 tablespoons lemon juice

1 clove garlic, minced or pressed

$1/2$ teaspoon ground cumin

$1/4$ teaspoon chili powder

2 turkey breast tenderloins (about 1 lb. *total*),
   cut into 1-inch pieces

$1/2$ cup golden raisins

$1/4$ cup dry white wine

2 medium-size carrots, cut into $1/4$-inch slanting
   slices

1 large onion (about 8 oz.), thinly sliced

2 teaspoons olive oil or salad oil

2 to 3 teaspoons curry powder

1 to 2 tablespoons chopped fresh mint or parsley

2 tablespoons salted roasted cashews, chopped

Mint or parsley sprigs

1 Prepare Coconut Rice. Meanwhile, in a large bowl, combine 1 tablespoon water, lemon juice, garlic, cumin, and chili powder. Add turkey and stir to coat. Set aside; stir occasionally. In a small bowl, combine raisins and wine; let stand until raisins are softened (about 10 minutes), stirring occasionally.

2 In a wide nonstick frying pan or wok, combine carrots, onion, and $1/4$ cup water. Cover and cook over medium-high heat until carrots are tender-crisp to bite (about 5 minutes). Uncover and stir-fry until liquid has evaporated. Remove vegetables from pan with a slotted spoon and keep warm.

3 Heat oil in pan. When oil is hot, add turkey mixture. Stir-fry just until meat is no longer pink in center; cut to test (3 to 4 minutes). Add water, 1 tablespoon at a time, if pan appears dry. Add curry powder and stir-fry just until fragrant (about 30 seconds; do not scorch).

4 Add raisins (and soaking liquid) to pan; return vegetables to pan. Bring to a boil; then boil, stirring, until liquid has evaporated (about 2 minutes). Remove from heat; stir in chopped mint and cashews. Spoon Coconut Rice into 4 wide bowls; top with turkey mixture and garnish with mint sprigs.

makes 4 servings

COCONUT RICE

In a 3- to 4-quart pan, combine 1 cup each water and low-fat milk. Bring just to a boil over medium- high heat. Stir in 1 cup long-grain white rice. Reduce heat, cover, and simmer until liquid has been absorbed and rice is tender to bite (about 20 minutes). Stir in $1/4$ cup sweetened shredded coconut. Keep warm until ready to serve, fluffing occasionally with a fork.

per serving: 502 calories, 36 g protein, 70 g carbohydrates, 7 g total fat, 72 mg cholesterol, 158 mg sodium

jalapeño chicken with mole poblano

preparation time: about 45 minutes

1 tablespoon sesame seeds

1 large onion, chopped

4 cloves garlic, minced or pressed

1 small very ripe banana, chopped

¼ cup chopped pitted prunes

2 tablespoons raisins

1 tablespoon creamy peanut butter

5 tablespoons unsweetened cocoa powder

3 tablespoons chili powder

2 teaspoons sugar

½ teaspoon ground cinnamon

⅛ teaspoon ground coriander

⅛ teaspoon ground cumin

⅛ teaspoon ground cloves

⅛ teaspoon anise seeds, crushed

2 cups fat-free reduced-sodium chicken broth

1 small can (about 6 oz.) tomato paste

8 skinless, boneless chicken breast halves
   (about 6 oz. *each*)

1 Toast sesame seeds in a wide nonstick frying pan over medium heat until golden (about 4 minutes), stirring often. Transfer to a bowl; set aside.

2 To pan, add onion, garlic, banana, prunes, raisins, peanut butter, and 3 tablespoons water. Cook over medium heat, stirring often, until mixture is richly browned (10 to 15 minutes); if pan appears dry, add more water, 1 tablespoon at a time. Stir in cocoa, chili powder, sugar, cinnamon, coriander, cumin, cloves, anise seeds, and ¾ cup of the broth. Bring mixture to a boil over medium-high heat.

3 Transfer hot onion mixture to a food processor or blender and add tomato paste, 2 teaspoons of the anise seeds, and a little of the remaining broth. Whirl until smoothly puréed; then stir in remaining broth. Cover and keep warm. (At this point, you may let cool; then cover and refrigerate for up to 3 days; freeze for longer storage. Reheat before continuing.)

4 While onion mixture is browning, rinse chicken and pat dry. Place jelly in a bowl and stir to soften; add chicken in a lightly oiled 10- by 15-inch rimmed baking pan. Bake in a 450° oven until meat in thickest part is no longer pink; cut to test (12 to 15 minutes).

5 To serve, spoon some of the warm mole sauce onto dinner plates; top with chicken, then more mole sauce. Sprinkle with remaining 1 teaspoon sesame seeds. Season to taste with salt; serve with lime wedges to squeeze over chicken to taste.

makes 8 servings

per serving: 264 calories, 34 g protein, 23 g carbohydrates, 6 g total fat, 74 mg cholesterol, 322 mg sodium

MICROWAVE A WHOLE FRYING CHICKEN: Remove neck and giblets; reserve for other uses, if desired. Discard lumps of fat. Rinse chicken inside and out, and pat dry. Stuff, if desired and close stuffed cavities with string and wooden picks (not metallic skewers). Place, breast down, on a nonmetallic rack in a 7 by 11-inch microwave-proof baking dish. Cover with heavy-duty plastic wrap or wax paper. For a 3- to 3 ½-pound bird, microwave on HIGH for 6 to 7 minutes per pound, turning chicken over and rotating dish a quarter turn halfway through cooking.

turkey chili

preparation time: about 55 minutes

1 tablespoon salad oil

1 pound skinned and boned turkey breast, cut into 1 1/2-inch chunks

1 medium-size onion, chopped

1 small green bell pepper, seeded and chopped

1 clove garlic, minced or pressed

1 small can (about 8 oz.) tomatoes, drained and chopped

2 cans (about 15 oz. *each*) kidney beans, drained

1 large can (15 oz.) no-salt-added tomato sauce

2 tablespoons reduced-sodium soy sauce

1 1/2 tablespoons chili powder

1/2 teaspoon *each* ground cumin, dry sage leaves, and dry thyme leaves

Garnishes (optional; suggestions follow)

1 Heat oil in a 12- to 14-inch frying pan over medium heat. Add turkey and cook, stirring often, until browned on all sides (about 6 minutes).

2 Remove turkey from pan. Add onion, bell pepper, and garlic; cook, stirring occasionally, until onion is soft (about 10 minutes). Add tomatoes, beans, tomato sauce, soy, chili powder, cumin, sage, and thyme. Bring to a boil. Then reduce heat, cover, and simmer until chili is thick and meat is no longer pink in center; cut to test (about 20 minutes; uncover for last 5 minutes).

3 Serve in bowls and accompany with garnishes.

makes 4 servings

GARNISHES

In separate bowls, offer 8 green onions (including tops), sliced; 1 cup chopped tomatoes; and 1/2 cup shredded jack cheese, if desired.

per serving: 407 calories, 40g protein, 47g carbohydrates, 7g total fat, 70 mg cholesterol, 1259 mg sodium

chicken kebabs shanghai

preparation time: about 40 minutes
marinating time: at least 30 minutes

3/4 teaspoon grated orange peel

1/3 cup orange juice

3 tablespoons firmly packed brown sugar

2 tablespoons reduced-sodium soy sauce

4 teaspoons *each* minced fresh ginger and red wine vinegar

1 tablespoon Asian sesame oil or salad oil

1/2 teaspoon ground coriander

1 1/2 pounds skinned, boned chicken breasts, cut into 1 1/2-inch chunks

1 medium-size pineapple, peeled, cored, and cut into 1-inch chunks

1 In a medium-size bowl, mix orange peel, orange juice, sugar, soy sauce, ginger, vinegar, oil, and coriander. Stir in chicken. Cover and refrigerate for at least 30 minutes or up to 2 hours.

2 Lift chicken from marinade and drain briefly; reserve marinade. Thread chicken and pineapple chunks on thin metal skewers, alternating 2 chicken chunks and one pineapple chunk. Brush reserved marinade over pineapple. Place skewers on a rack in a 12- by 15-inch broiler pan. Broil about 4 inches below heat, turning once, until chicken is no longer pink in center; cut to test (about 12 minutes).

makes 4 to 6 servings

per serving: 299 calories, 33 g protein, 319 carbohydrates, 5 g total fat, 79 mg cholesterol, 333 mg sodium

picadillo stew

preparation time: about 40 minutes

2 tablespoons slivered almonds

1/4 cup dry red wine

2 tablespoons reduced sodium soy sauce

1 tablespoon lemon juice

2 teaspoons sugar

1 teaspoon *each* ground cumin, ground coriander, and chili powder

1/8 teaspoon ground cinnamon

4 teaspoons cornstarch

1 teaspoon salad oil

1 pound boneless turkey breast, cut into 1-inch chunks

1 large onion, chopped

2 cloves garlic, minced or pressed

1 can (about 14 1/2 oz.) tomatoes

2/3 cup raisins

Pepper

1 Toast almonds in a small flying pan over medium heat until golden (5 to 7 minutes), stirring often. Transfer almonds to a bowl and set aside.

2 In a small bowl, mix wine, soy sauce, lemon juice, sugar, cumin, coriander, chili powder, cinnamon, and cornstarch until smooth. Set aside.

3 Heat oil in a wide nonstick frying pan or 5-quart pan over high heat. Add turkey, onion, and garlic. Cook, stirring, until meat is no longer pink in thickest part; cut to test (10 to 15 minutes). Add water, 1 tablespoon at a time, if pan appears dry. Add tomatoes and their liquid (break tomatoes up with a spoon), wine mixture, and raisins to pan. Bring to a boil; boil, stirring, just until thickened.

4 To serve, ladle stew into bowls and sprinkle with almonds. Season to taste with pepper.

makes 4 servings

per serving: 317 calories, 32 g protein, 36 g carbohydrates, 5 g total fat, 70 mg cholesterol, 538 mg sodium

strawberry chicken

preparation time: about 10 minutes
baking time: about 45 minutes

1 can (about 8 oz.) tomato sauce

1 cup strawberry jam

2 tablespoons red wine vinegar

1 tablespoon chili powder

1/2 teaspoon *each* dry thyme and ground ginger

12 skinless chicken thighs (2 to 2 1/4 lbs. *total*) trimmed of fat

Salt

3 cups hot cooked a short-grain rice

1/2 cup thinly sliced green onions

1 In a shallow 3-quart casserole, mix tomato sauce, jam, vinegar, chili powder, thyme, and ginger.

2 Rinse chicken and pat dry; then add to sauce and turn to coat. Bake in a 400° oven, basting occasionally, until meat near bone is no longer pink; cut to test (about 45 minutes). Season to taste with salt.

3 Spoon rice onto a platter. Top with chicken, sauce, and onions.

makes 4 to 6 servings

per serving: 505 calories, 33 g protein, 81 g carbohydrates, 6 g total fat, 118 mg cholesterol, 441 mg sodium

chicken curry in pita bread

preparation time: about 40 minutes

1/2 **cup raisins or dried currants**

1 cup plain nonfat yogurt

2 tablespoons cornstarch

2 teaspoons olive oil

12 ounces skinless, boneless chicken breast, cut into 1/2**-inch pieces**

1 medium-size onion, chopped

2 cloves garlic, minced or pressed

2 teaspoons curry powder

1/2 **cup apricot jam or preserves**

Salt and pepper

1 medium-size cucumber, very thinly sliced

4 pita breads (*each* about 6 inches in diameter), cut crosswise into halves

1 In a small bowl, combine raisins and 1/4 cup water; let stand until raisins are softened (about 10 minutes), stirring occasionally. Meanwhile, in another small bowl, stir together yogurt and cornstarch until smoothly blended; set aside.

2 Heat oil in a wide nonstick frying pan or wok over medium-high heat. When oil is hot, add chicken and 1 tablespoon water. Stir-fry until meat is no longer pink in center; cut to test (3 to 4 minutes). Remove chicken from pan with a slotted spoon and keep warm. Discard drippings from pan.

3 Add onion, garlic, curry powder, and 1/4 cup water to pan; stir-fry until onion is soft (about 4 minutes; do not scorch). Add water, 1 tablespoon at a time, if pan appears dry. Add raisins (and soaking water) and jam. Bring to a boil; then boil, stirring, until almost all liquid has evaporated (5 to 7 minutes). Reduce heat to medium-low; stir in chicken and yogurt mixture. Simmer gently, stirring constantly, until sauce is slightly thickened (do not boil). Season to taste with salt and pepper.

4 To serve, divide cucumber slices equally among pita halves; fill pitas equally with chicken mixture.

makes 4 servings

per serving: 506 calories, 30 g protein, 88 g carbohydrates, 5 g total fat, 51 mg cholesterol, 442 mg sodium

chicken-stuffed melon with raspberries

preparation time: about 45 minutes

Lime-Honey Dressing (recipe follows)

1 1/2 **pounds skinned and boned chicken breasts**

4 cups water

2 large cantaloupes

1 cup seedless green grapes

2 kiwi fruit, peeled and sliced

1 cup raspberries

1 Prepare dressing; set aside. Rinse and drain chicken. In a 4- to 5-quart pan, bring water to a boil over high heat. Add chicken, cover pan, and remove from heat. Let stand, covered, until chicken is no longer pink in thickest part; cut to test (about 20 minutes). Drain chicken and place in ice water until cool; drain again. Cut into 1/2-inch chunks.

2 Cut each cantaloupe in half, making zigzag cuts. Scoop out and discard seeds. With a curved grapefruit knife, cut fruit from rind, then cut into 1/2-inch chunks. Drain melon pieces and shells.

3 In a bowl, combine melon, chicken, and grapes; spoon into shells. Top with kiwi slices, raspberries, and dressing.

makes 4 servings

LIME-HONEY DRESSING

Stir together 1/2 cup each lime juice and honey with 1/2 teaspoon each ground coriander and ground nutmeg.

per serving: 340 calories, 29 g protein, 55 g carbohydrates, 3 g total fat, 66 mg cholesterol, 101 mg sodium

saffron & honey chicken

preparation time: about 1 hour

2/3 cup low-sodium chicken broth

2 tablespoons *each* lime juice and honey

1/4 teaspoon saffron threads

1 teaspoon white Worcestershire

2 teaspoons curry powder

1/2 teaspoon dry oregano

1/4 teaspoon paprika

1/8 teaspoon pepper

2 teaspoons reduced-sodium soy sauce

2 tablespoons white rice flour blended with
  1/4 cup cold water

6 *each* chicken drumsticks and thighs (about
  3 lbs. *total*), skinned and trimmed of fat

Chopped parsley

1 In a 1 1/2- to 2-quart pan, stir together broth, lime juice, honey, saffron, Worcestershire, curry powder, oregano, paprika, pepper, and soy sauce. Bring to a boil over high heat; then reduce heat and simmer, uncovered, stirring occasionally, until reduced to 1/2 cup (about 15 minutes). Stir in rice flour mixture; bring to a boil over high heat, stirring. Remove from heat.

2 Rinse chicken, pat dry, and arrange, skinned side up, in a 9- by 13-inch baking pan. Spoon sauce evenly over chicken. Cover and bake in a 375° oven until meat near bone is no longer pink; cut to test (about 35 minutes).

3 Transfer chicken to a platter; stir sauce to blend, then spoon over chicken. Sprinkle with parsley.

makes 6 servings

per serving: 198 calories, 27 g protein, 10 g carbohydrates, 5 g total fat, 104 mg cholesterol, 193 mg sodium

chicken and black bean bake

preparation time: about 35 minutes

1 package (about 7 oz.) or 1 2/3 cups instant
  refried black bean mix

2 cups boiling water

1/3 to 1/2 cup dry sherry or water

4 boneless, skinless chicken breast halves (about
  1 1/2 lbs. total)

8 cups shredded iceberg lettuce

1/2 cup shredded jack cheese

1 fresh red or green jalapeño chile, thinly sliced
  crosswise (optional)

Cherry tomatoes

Reduced-fat sour cream

1 In a shallow 2- to 2 1/2-quart baking dish, combine refried bean mix, boiling water, and sherry (use the 1/2-cup amount if you prefer a saucelike consistency). Rinse chicken and pat dry; then arrange, skinned side up, atop beans. Bake in a 400° oven until meat in thickest part is no longer pink; cut to test (about 20 minutes). Stir any liquid that accumulates around chicken into beans.

2 Mound lettuce equally on 4 individual plates; top with beans and chicken. Sprinkle with cheese and chile (if used); garnish with cherry tomatoes. Offer sour cream to add to taste.

makes 4 servings

per serving: 469 calories, 54 g protein, 36 g carbohydrates, 8 g total fat, 114 mg cholesterol, 597 mg sodium

sake-steamed chicken

preparation time: about 30 minutes
marinating time: at least 30 minutes

$1/2$ **cup sake or unseasoned rice vinegar**

$1/2$ **teaspoon salt**

6 boneless, skinless chicken breast halves (about 2 $1/4$ lbs. *total*)

1 small head iceberg lettuce

About $1/3$ cup reduced-sodium soy sauce

1 tablespoon prepared horseradish

Lemon wedges

3 cups hot cooked rice

$1/2$ **cup thinly sliced green onions**

1 In a medium-size bowl, stir together sake and salt until salt is dissolved. Rinse chicken and pat dry; add to marinade and turn to coat. Cover and refrigerate for at least 30 minutes or up to 2 hours.

2 Lift chicken from bowl and drain briefly; discard marinade. Arrange chicken, with thickest parts toward outside, in a single layer in a 10- to 11-inch round heatproof nonmetal dish. Cover with wax paper or foil and set on a rack in a large pan above 1 inch of boiling water. Cover and steam, keeping water at a steady boil, until meat in thickest part is no longer pink; cut to test (about 12 minutes).

3 Meanwhile, place 1 or 2 large lettuce leaves on each of 6 individual plates. Finely shred remaining lettuce; mound atop leaves. Divide soy sauce among 6 tiny dipping bowls; add $1/2$ teaspoon of the horseradish to each, then place bowls on plates. Place a few lemon wedges on each plate.

4 Cut chicken crosswise into $1/2$-inch-wide strips. Spoon rice and chicken over lettuce; sprinkle with onions. To eat, squeeze lemon into soy mixture. Dip chicken into sauce. Or tear lettuce leaves into pieces and fill with chicken, rice, and shredded lettuce; season with sauce and eat out of hand.

makes 6 servings

per serving: 360 calories, 44 g protein, 35 g carbohydrates, 3 g total fat, 99 mg cholesterol, 742 mg sodium

apple turkey loaf

preparation time: about 25 minutes
baking time: about 1 hour

1 tablespoon butter or margarine

2 medium-size tart green-skinned apples, cored and chopped

1 medium-size onion, chopped

1 $1/2$ pounds ground skinless turkey breast

1 $1/2$ teaspoons dry marjoram

1 teaspoon *each* dry thyme, dry sage, and pepper

$1/2$ **cup chopped parsley**

2 large egg whites (about $1/4$ cup)

$1/2$ **cup *each* fine dry bread crumbs and nonfat milk**

1 Melt butter in a wide frying pan over medium heat. Add apples and onion. Cook, stirring occasionally, until onion is soft (about 7 minutes). Remove from heat and let cool; then spoon into a large bowl. Add turkey, marjoram, thyme, sage, pepper, parsley, egg whites, bread crumbs, and milk; mix lightly.

2 Pat turkey mixture into a 5- by 9-inch loaf pan. Bake in a 350° oven until browned on top and no longer pink in center; cut to test (about 1 hour). Drain and discard fat from pan, then invert pan and turn loaf out onto a platter. Serve loaf hot; or let cool, then cover and refrigerate for up to 1 day.

makes 6 servings

per serving: 237 calories, 32 g protein, 19 g carbohydrates, 3 g total fat, 76 mg cholesterol, 185 mg sodium

sesame chicken with stir-fry vegetables

preparation time: about 35 minutes

4 chicken breast halves (about 2 lbs. *total*), skinned and boned

1 teaspoon sesame seeds vegetable oil cooking spray

4 teaspoons rice vinegar

4 teaspoons reduced-sodium soy sauce

1 1/2 teaspoons Asian sesame oil

1 tablespoon grated fresh ginger

2 cloves garlic, minced or pressed 1/2 teaspoon sugar

1 tablespoon vegetable oil

8 ounces mushrooms, sliced

4 cups thinly sliced red cabbage

4 ounces Chinese pea pods (also called snow peas), ends and strings removed

2 cups hot cooked rice

1 Rinse chicken, pat dry, and sprinkle with sesame seeds. Spray a ridged cooktop grill pan with cooking spray. Place over medium heat and preheat until a drop of water dances on surface. Then place chicken on grill and cook, turning once, until well browned on outside and no longer pink in thickest part; cut to test (12 to 15 minutes).

2 Meanwhile, in a small bowl, stir together vinegar, soy sauce, sesame oil, ginger, garlic, and sugar; set aside. Then heat vegetable oil in a wide nonstick frying pan or wok over medium-high heat.

3 Add mushrooms and cook, stirring often, for about 3 minutes. Add cabbage and cook, stirring often, until it begins to soften (about 2 minutes). Add pea pods and cook, stirring, just until they turn bright green (1 to 2 minutes). Add vinegar mixture and stir for 1 more minute.

4 Divide vegetables among 4 warm dinner plates. Cut each chicken piece diagonally across the grain into 1/2-inch-wide strips. Arrange chicken over vegetables; serve with rice.

makes 4 servings

per serving: 400 calories, 40 g protein, 40 g carbohydrates, 8 g total fat, 86 mg cholesterol, 310 mg sodium

white wine turkey loaf

preparation time: about 1 hour

1/3 cup low-sodium chicken broth

1/3 cup thinly sliced green onions (including tops)

1 small green bell pepper, stemmed, seeded, and diced

1/2 cup dry white wine

1 cup soft whole wheat bread crumbs

1 teaspoon dry thyme leaves

1 pound fresh ground turkey

1 egg white

Freshly ground pepper

1 can (8 oz.) no-salt-added tomato sauce

1 In a small frying pan, bring chicken broth to a boil over high heat. Add onions and bell pepper and cook, stirring, until liquid has evaporated and vegetables are soft (about 5 minutes). Add wine, bring to a boil, and remove from heat. Stir in bread crumbs and thyme.

2 In a bowl, mix turkey, bread crumb mixture, and egg white; season to taste with pepper. Pat mixture into a 5- by 9-inch loaf pan. Spread half the tomato sauce over meat.

3 Bake in a 350° oven for 30 minutes. Remove pan from oven and tip to pour off fat. Spread remaining tomato sauce over loaf and continue baking until meat in center is no longer pink; cut to test (10 to 15 more minutes). Let stand for 5 minutes before slicing.

makes 4 to 6 servings

per serving: 207 calories, 19 g protein, 10 g carbohydrates, 10 g total fat, 46 mg cholesterol, 134 mg sodium

broccoli-stuffed chicken breasts

preparation time: about 1 hour

1 tablespoon salad oil

1/2 cup minced shallots

1 pound mushrooms, minced

2 cups broccoli flowerets

2 tablespoons Madeira

2 tablespoons grated Parmesan cheese

1/2 cup shredded reduced-fat Jarlsberg or Swiss cheese

6 boneless, skinless chicken breast halves (about 2 1/4 lbs. *total*)

1 Heat oil in a wide frying pan over medium heat. Add shallots and mushrooms; cook, stirring occasionally, until shallots are soft (about 5 minutes). Add broccoli and Madeira; cover and cook, stirring occasionally, until broccoli is tender-crisp to bite (about 5 minutes). Remove from heat and stir in Parmesan cheese and 1/4 cup of the Jarlsberg cheese. Let cool.

2 Rinse chicken and pat dry. Place each breast half between 2 sheets of plastic wrap and pound with a flat-surfaced mallet to a thickness of about 1/4 inch. In center of each pounded chicken piece, mound a sixth of the broccoli-mushroom mixture. Roll chicken around filling to enclose. Set chicken rolls, seam side down, in a greased 9- by 13-inch baking pan. Sprinkle evenly with remaining 1/4 cup Jarlsberg cheese.

3 Bake in a 450° oven until meat is no longer pink and filling is hot in center; cut to test (about 15 minutes). Then broil 4 to 6 inches below heat until cheese is browned (about 2 minutes).

makes 6 servings

per serving: 291 calories, 46 g protein, 9 g carbohydrates, 7 g total fat, 105 mg cholesterol, 190 mg sodium

chicken capocollo

preparation time: about 30 minutes

4 small boneless, skinless chicken breast halves (about 1 lb. *total*)

4 thin slices capocollo (or coppa) sausage or prosciutto (about 1 oz. *total*)

2 teaspoons olive oil

4 green onions, thinly sliced

2 cloves garlic, minced or pressed

1/4 cup low-sodium chicken broth or dry white wine

2 tablespoons Dijon mustard

1 tablespoon lemon juice

1/2 teaspoon dry basil

1 Rinse chicken and pat dry. Place each breast half between 2 sheets of plastic wrap and pound with a flat-surfaced mallet to a thickness of 1/3 to 1/2 inch. Lay a slice of capocollo on each pounded chicken piece, pressing lightly so that chicken and sausage stick together. Set aside.

2 Heat oil in a wide frying pan over medium heat. Add onions and garlic; cook, stirring often, until vegetables are lightly browned (about 3 minutes). Then push vegetables to one side and place chicken in pan. Cook just until edges of chicken pieces begin to brown on bottom (about 4 minutes). Turn pieces over and continue to cook until meat in thickest part is no longer pink; cut to test (3 to 4 more minutes). Transfer chicken, sausage side up, to a platter; keep warm.

3 To pan, add broth, mustard, lemon juice, and basil. Bring to a boil over high heat, stirring constantly; then pour broth mixture over chicken.

makes 4 servings

per serving: 180 calories, 29 g protein, 3 g carbohydrates, 5 g total fat, 72 mg cholesterol, 437 mg sodium

roast turkey breasts & four drumsticks

preparation time: about 45 minutes
roasting time: about 2 1/4 hours

1 boneless turkey breast half (3 to 3 1/2 lbs.)

4 turkey drumsticks (about 1 lb. *each*)

2/3 cup apple, quince, or red currant jelly

2 tablespoons raspberry vinegar or red wine vinegar

1/2 teaspoon ground sage

Dried Tomato Couscous (recipe follows)

2 tablespoons cornstarch

about 2 cups low-sodium chicken broth

Salt and pepper

1 Trim and discard fat from turkey breast. Rinse breast and drumsticks; pat dry. Set breast skin side up and fold narrow end under to make an evenly thick piece; pull skin to cover as much of meat as possible. Using cotton string, tie breast snugly at 1-inch intervals lengthwise and crosswise. Set all turkey aside.

2 In a small pan, combine jelly, vinegar, and sage. Stir over medium heat until jelly is melted.

3 Arrange drumsticks slightly apart in an 11- by 17-inch roasting pan; brush with some of the jelly mixture. Roast in a 375° oven for 15 minutes. Set breast in pan and brush with jelly mixture. Continue to roast until a meat thermometer inserted in thickest part of breast registers 165° and until thermometer inserted in thickest part of drumsticks registers 185° (about 2 hours). If some pieces are done before others, remove them from oven and keep warm. As turkey roasts, baste it with pan drippings and jelly mixture, using all. If drippings begin to scorch, add 1/3 cup water and stir to scrape browned bits free.

4 About 30 minutes before turkey is done, prepare Dried Tomato Couscous.

5 When turkey is done, transfer it to a carving board, cover lightly, and let stand for about 10 minutes. As juices accumulate on board, drain them into roasting pan.

6 To make gravy, skim and discard fat from pan drippings. Pour drippings into a 1-quart or larger glass measure; smoothly blend in cornstarch. Then add enough broth to make 2 1/2 cups. Return mixture to roasting pan; bring to a boil over high heat, stirring. Season to taste with salt and pepper. Pour into a bowl or gravy boat. To serve, remove strings from turkey breast, then thinly slice meat across the grain. Slice drumsticks or serve whole. Arrange turkey on platter around couscous; accompany with gravy.

makes 12 to 16 servings

DRIED TOMATO COUSCOUS

Soak 1/2 cup dried tomatoes in 5 cups boiling water until very soft (about 30 minutes). Drain tomatoes, pressing out excess liquid and reserving all soaking water. Chop tomatoes coarsely and set aside. In a 3 1/2- to 4-quart pan, combine water from tomatoes and 1 can (about 14 1/2 oz.) low-sodium chicken broth. Bring to a boil over high heat. Stir in tomatoes, 1/2 teaspoon dry oregano, 1/4 teaspoon dry sage, and 3 cups couscous. Cover pan, remove from heat, and let stand for about 5 minutes. Fluff couscous with a fork; mound on a large platter, allowing room for turkey.

per serving: 465 calories, 50 g protein, 44 g carbohydrates, 8 g total fat, 127 mg cholesterol, 124 mg sodium

index